So You Want to . . .

Be a

Fashion

Designer

Here's the Info You Need

D1368158

by Lisa McGinnes

Foreword by Maya Ramirez,
winner of *Project Runway Junior*

SO YOU WANT TO . . . BE A FASHION DESIGNER: HERE'S THE INFO YOU NEED

1405 SW 6th Avenue • Ocala, Florida 34471 • Phone 800-814-1132 • Fax 352-622-1875
Website: www.atlantic-pub.com • Email: sales@atlantic-pub.com
SAN Number: 268-1250

Library of Congress Cataloging-in-Publication Data

Names: McGinnes, Lisa.
Title: So you want to be a fashion designer : here's the info you need / by Lisa McGinnes.
Description: Ocala, Florida : Atlantic Publishing Group, Inc., [2016] | Includes bibliographical references and index.
Identifiers: LCCN 2016057501 (print) | LCCN 2016058098 (ebook) | ISBN 9781620232057 (alk. paper) | ISBN 1620232057 (alk. paper) | ISBN 9781620232064 (ebook)
Subjects: LCSH: Fashion design—Vocational guidance.
Classification: LCC TT507 .M326 2016 (print) | LCC TT507 (ebook) | DDC 746.9/2023—dc23
LC record available at https://lccn.loc.gov/2016057501

PROJECT MANAGER AND EDITOR: Rebekah Sack • rsack@atlantic-pub.com
ASSISTANT EDITOR: Cathie Bucci • cathiebucci@yahoo.com
INTERIOR LAYOUT AND JACKET DESIGN: Nicole Sturk • nicolejonessturk@gmail.com
COVER DESIGN: Jackie Miller • millerjackiej@gmail.com

Reduce. Reuse.
RECYCLE.

A decade ago, Atlantic Publishing signed the Green Press Initiative. These guidelines promote environmentally friendly practices, such as using recycled stock and vegetable-based inks, avoiding waste, choosing energy-efficient resources, and promoting a no-pulping policy. We now use 100-percent recycled stock on all our books. The results: in one year, switching to post-consumer recycled stock saved 24 mature trees, 5,000 gallons of water, the equivalent of the total energy used for one home in a year, and the equivalent of the greenhouse gases from one car driven for a year.

Over the years, we have adopted a number of dogs from rescues and shelters. First there was Bear and after he passed, Ginger and Scout. Now, we have Kira, another rescue. They have brought immense joy and love not just into our lives, but into the lives of all who met them.

We want you to know a portion of the profits of this book will be donated in Bear, Ginger and Scout's memory to local animal shelters, parks, conservation organizations, and other individuals and nonprofit organizations in need of assistance.

– Douglas & Sherri Brown,
President & Vice-President of Atlantic Publishing

Table of Contents

Foreword

Fashion has not always been something I was interested in. When I was little, I was very much a sporty girl. My mom made me wear dresses, and eventually, I started to like them. I learned how to sew in the third grade by watching YouTube videos, and I fell in love with the art form. I really love making gowns and more formal pieces, because I find it the most rewarding to transform people through clothing.

I am self-taught, so I worked my way up to auditioning for *Project Runway Junior*. I auditioned through an online application. The casting group was called mystic art pictures, and they had a step-by-step online application. After that, I got a call back and went to New York City. It was so much fun to show my pieces in front of real designers. After that, I got a call telling me I made it on the show!

It was one of the most incredible experiences of my life. I learned a lot about time management, perseverance, friendship, family, and just how far I can push myself. *Project Runway* allowed me to grow immensely as a designer and as a person. I am very interested in high-end women's wear.

For others who want to follow in my path, practice doesn't make perfect, but it does make you better. If you really love it, then devote time and passion to it. I currently am working on a new collection that is also a new direction for me. Don't be afraid to play around with your style. Ultimately, I want to have a big brand with storefronts and runway shows, so my ultimate advice is to dream as big as you can, and then make it happen!

—Maya Ramirez, aspiring high-end women's wear designer

Maya Ramirez, 15 years old, is the winner of the first season of *Project Runway Junior*. Visit her website at **www.mayarene.com**.

Introduction

Some people select their clothes based on comfort, color, or (gasp!) what's on sale—relying on magazine ads, social media, or the department store merchandisers to tell them what to wear.

Not you, fashionista.

You get a notification on your phone when Vogue releases the *Best Dressed of the Week* and when @whowhatwear posts on Instagram. You have your entire wardrobe loaded onto the Stylebook app.

You don't just stay on top of fashion, you *make* fashion! You can put together an #OOTD better than anyone. So . . . what do you need to know to make your passion a reality? Let's delve in to the world of style and discover what you need to know to cultivate your own fashion empire.

Chapter One
An Overview of Fashion Design

A Whirlwind History of Fashion

Fashion design made its debut as a career around 1800 when couturiers were dressing France's aristocrats. European design houses ruled the world of fashion until U.S. designers brought ready-to-wear to American women after World War II.

In the second half of the 20th century, American designers finally made their mark. Hollywood celebrities influenced trends from the era of the hippie through glam rock and grunge. Calvin Klein and Ralph Lauren found worldwide success.

By the start of the 21st century, fewer Americans were employed in the fashion industry as manufacturing became more mechanized and more operations moved overseas.

However, today's technology has opened up new career opportunities with titles like Apparel Engineer and Computer-Aided Design Specialist. Although employment in fashion design is growing more slowly than many other professions, the fashion technology industry has been sparked by media attention on fashion, home décor, and weddings. In today's world where most people can't even sew on a button, some low-tech jobs like Alterationists are making a comeback.

How Much Money Will You Make?

In 2015, the median salary for a fashion designer in the U.S. was $63,670, which is well above average salaries across all fields. That figure can vary greatly depending on experience, popularity, and location. Salaries for an entry-level position in fashion design can be as low as minimum wage, and many high-end designers make well over $100,000 a year.[1]

Where Are the Jobs?

If you want to be in the heart of American couture, no place comes close to New York City.

Fast Fact

Southern California/Hollywood is the second-largest fashion locale.

For designers who don't want to move to either coast, there are a few smaller fashion houses in places like Miami, home of Swim Fashion Week. Designers working with department stores may be employed in locations like Dallas, Texas, at Neiman Marcus headquarters, or Columbus, Ohio, home of Victoria's Secret. The increased popularity of outdoor and athletic wear has created more jobs with companies like Columbia Sportswear and The North Face headquartered in the Pacific Northwest.

Of course, with so many online platforms to market your designs directly to consumers, you can work from anywhere that has an internet connection!

1. Bureau of Labor Statistics, 2015

Do You Have What it Takes?

A designer is a creative genius. You're an artist, you can sketch an idea, and you have an eye for colors and lines. You know details, like the difference between a knife pleat and a box pleat. Just don't overlook some basic, non-design skills that will help you reach your goals.

"Be prepared to be bombarded by harsh criticism and nit-picky opinions whether you asked for it or not. I've been told my shoulders are weird, to stand in the non-speaking line at a casting because I have a slight lisp, and that I should wax my arms. (My arms were once Nair-ed on set. Talk about embarrassing.)**"**

— **Lindsey Crown**, 4-year Top 10 agency-signed model

Communication

Communication skills are important in pretty much any profession, and fashion design is no different. Even Fashion Institute of Technology's associate degree program in fashion design requires a communication course.

As a designer, you need to communicate important information with clients and potential clients, so it's important to have good speaking, listening, and writing skills. You need be able to understand what the client wants, even when they can't articulate it. You'll have to talk to the retail buyers who can get your designs into department stores and boutiques, the suppliers who sell you fabric and accessories, and the contractors who will sew your final creations.

Perseverance

❝Don't expect to get featured on Vogue right away; everything takes time.**❞**

—**Monil Kothari**, Founder of Antandre,
a jewelry e-commerce company

Even if you're whipping up one-of-a-kind creations in your room and selling them online, creating a line of clothing takes time. A lot of time. It's a process—you figure out your design, put it on paper, make a pattern, choose the fabric, sew a prototype, make changes (and more changes), and finally construct the final garment. Until you have a name in the fashion industry, you're always working to find your niche and build clientele.

Did You Know?

In some apparel companies, the process of turning a design concept into a finished garment can take up to two years.

Organization

As you try to break out as a designer, you'll be juggling a lot of information—multiple clients, designs, and deadlines. Figuring out a system to keep sketches, fabrics, and paperwork organized will save you time (like when Marc Jacobs calls and wants to interview you right now!).

Besides all your creative materials, you're actually running a business, so you have to manage financial information, contracts, and marketing data, too.

Technical skills

Just like every industry, fashion design has gone high tech. The sketches that got Coco Chanel into the business in the early 1900s won't get you very far today. Yes, you still need to know how to sketch, but being proficient with industry-specific software can help you get the edge over other job applicants (and there will be a lot of competition!). A working knowledge of art design software like Adobe Illustrator and computer-aided drafting (CAD) programs will give you a good foundation if you don't have access to fashion-specific design software right now.

Even if you don't plan to personally make the garments you design, you should still know enough about sewing and patternmaking to work with your construction staff. You will need to be able to tell them exactly what needs to be done to get the look you're after.

Creativity

Fashion is a crowded field. There are a lot of designers competing for the same retail and wholesale customers. Landing a big contract is hard for the new guy or girl, because some buyers prefer to work with established firms with proven track records.

That's why you have to stand out (and, to be honest, you probably already do). If you have a unique voice within the industry, then you have a better chance of attracting clients. To be successful, you can't just respond to trends—you have to *make* them. You wouldn't be interested in fashion design if you weren't a pretty creative individual, but you'll have to take big risks to get big rewards. And creativity isn't only important in your designs; the more innovative you are in marketing your business, the better your chances are of being discovered.

Did You Know?

Sebastian Professional hair care company sponsored London Fashion Week's first guerilla fashion show in 2015 to showcase up-and-coming designers.

Chapter Two

Paths to A Fashion Design Career

While very few designers have been lucky enough to work their way up in the industry without a formal education, most American fashion designers have a bachelor's degree in fashion design or fashion merchandising. Some designers have done well with a more generalized art degree, and some costume designers recommend a theater degree.

You know you can immerse yourself in fashion from day one by attending New York City's well-known Fashion Institute of Technology or Parsons School of Design.

But if you can't relocate to NYC just yet, you want to get a more well-rounded liberal arts education, or you only have the cash to attend a state school close to home, there are a handful of universities and even some community and technical colleges with accredited fashion programs throughout the country.

High school students in Orlando, Florida, can actually complete a fashion technology certificate through Orange Technical College's dual enrollment program with free (yes, free!) tuition. This unique program allows students to graduate from high school with 24 credits already earned toward an associate degree, and it offers five different specialties.[2]

See the chart below for a few random examples of this and other college programs in places you might not expect:

School	Location	Website	Degrees Offered	Name of Program	Comments
University of Minnesota	St. Paul, MN	Umn.edu	Bachelor of Science Master of Science Ph.D.	Apparel Design	Home of Wearable Product Design Center high-tech research labs

2. Orange Technical College, 2016

School	Location	Website	Degrees Offered	Name of Program	Comments
Iowa State University	Ames, IA	iastate.edu	Bachelor of Science	Apparel, Merchandising and Design	Design studio features cutting-edge technology including 3-D body scanner
University of Alabama	Tuscaloosa, AL	ua.edu	Bachelor of Science	Human Environmental Sciences – Apparel Design concentration	Check out the list of successful graduates on the website
California State University	Various locations in CA	calstate.edu	2-year certificate Bachelor of Arts Master of Arts	Art - Fashion and Textiles	L.A. program offers 2-yr certificates Long Beach program offers summer study in Paris
Rocky Mountain College of Art & Design	Lakewood, CO	rmcad.edu	Bachelor of Fine Arts	Fashion Apparel	Offers most classes on campus and online
Orange Technical College	Orlando, FL	orangetechcollege.net	Certificate -plus- 24 credits earned toward associate degree	Fashion Technology and Production	Specializations: • Patternmaker • Menswear • Lingerie • Formal wear • Alterations

One place to start looking at college options is the accrediting agency for fashion design programs—the National Association of Schools of Art and

Design. They list more than 100 accredited programs on their website (**www.nasad.org**).

Once you have that diploma in hand, you'll still need every advantage you can get to land your first job. One way to stand out from the competition is with additional certifications. Orange Technical College recommends that graduates apply for the National Sewing and Design Professional Certification through the Association of Sewing Design Professionals, Inc. They also offer two optional certifications:

1. Apparel and Textile Production and Merchandising certificate from the National Occupational Competency Testing Institute (NOCTI)

2. Adobe Certified Expert (Illustrator) certificate from Adobe Systems

Hopefully, you can start your fashion education before you even get to college with a summer program. If you're lucky enough to live in New York City (or can convince your parents to send you there for a week or two), Fashion Camp NYC (**www.fashioncampnyc.com**) has programs for aspiring designers ages 12-18 to learn the business from industry experts.

If they're not willing to send you to NYC for the summer but are willing to shell out a few hundred dollars, you can earn a Certificate in Fashion Design from Parsons School of Design without leaving home. You can access the 42-hour online course they launched with Teen Vogue in 2015 right from your laptop (**http://enroll-teenvogue.parsons.edu/online-fashion-courses**).

"When I was researching on furthering my education in a fashion institute internationally, I made sure to look at different fashion institutes in the fashion capitals of the world and what they were offering.

Here is a list of some of the best fashion colleges:

- Central Saint Martins, London, UK
- Royal College of Arts, London, UK
- London College of Fashion, London, UK
- Kingston University, London, UK
- Fashion Institute of Technology, New York, USA
- Parsons School of Design, New York, USA
- Royal Academy of Arts, Antwerp, Belgium
- Istituto Marangoni, Milan, Italy
- Bunga Fashion College, Tokyo, Japan
- Shenkar College of Engineering, Design and Art, Ramat Gan, Israel

Fashion is a more of a lifestyle choice, so being in a city like New York, Paris, London, Tokyo, or Milan enhances the learning process by many folds."

— **Sandhya Garg**, fashion designer
and *Project Runway* participant

Your Portfolio

Do you have a portfolio? If not, you're going to need one soon. London College of Fashion calls your portfolio a "visual representation of interests, exploration, experimentation, development and final pieces."[3] Your portfolio is *you* on paper, and it will be at least as important as your diploma or your résumé. This ever-changing collection of your best sketches and looks may be required for design school applications and will go with you to every job interview.

3. London College of Fashion, 2016

It's hard to know how to create your first portfolio. If you need one for a design school application, your school may give you specific instructions on what they are looking for. Take a look at college websites like Fashion Institute of Technology (**www.fit.edu**), Cornell University (**www.cornell.edu**), and London College of Fashion (**www.arts.ac.uk/fashion**), for helpful guides. Start with your art teacher—ask for advice and feedback.

Design Competitions

An education in design might be the most common path to a fashion design career, but it will still be a long road to success. If you want to skyrocket your career directly to the top, just win a design competition!

Project Runway Junior

After 14 seasons, the Lifetime channel's popular *Project Runway* fashion design competition reality show launched *Project Runway Junior* for designers ages 13-17. The first season winner in 2015 received a full scholarship to the Fashion Institute of Design & Merchandising in California, a complete home sewing and crafting studio provided by Brother, a feature in Seventeen Magazine, a $25,000 cash prize to help launch her line, and a Visionworks shopping spree. The youngest participant was also the first winner. Maya Ramirez of Toledo, Ohio, turned 14 during the show.

Did You Know?

Maya Ramirez, the 14-year-old winner of *Project Runway Junior*, taught herself how to sew watching YouTube videos! Read more of her story in the foreword of this book.

H&M Design Award

When you graduate from fashion school, you'll have more opportunities to apply to competitions, like the H&M Design Award. The fashion retailer started the competition in 2015 to "bring up the most promising talents in fashion and give them a springboard in their careers."[4] Not only do winners receive a 50,000-euro prize, but they get to develop pieces from their collection to be part of the H&M line.

LVMH Prize

The crown jewel of fashion competitions is the one presented by the European luxury goods conglomerate founded by Louis Vuitton. Their 15 fashion design houses include Marc Jacobs and Dior. In 2014, they awarded their first prize to a promising recent design school graduate. The young fashion designers' competition is open to designers under 40 who have produced at least two collections.

The prize is a grant of 300,000 euros (around $334,000) and personalized technical and financial support from the group of fashion experts for one year. This priceless mentoring opportunity covers all the areas of expertise that are critical to a young fashion brand — intellectual property, sourcing, production and distribution, image and advertising, marketing, and more.

"Fortunately, there are several prestigious fashion competitions in the world that can catapult a relatively new designer into a coveted brand in a short amount of time.

Here is a list of annual top fashion design competitions in the world:

- Vogue Fashion Fund

4. H&M, 2016

- LVMH Prize

- CFDA+ Design Graduates

- H & M Design Award

- World of Wearable Arts Awards

- International Woolmark Prize

- Project Runway

Also, Vogue Magazine is the fashion bible for many fashion designers, and Vogue Fashion Fund, the annual fashion competition for young brands, is like the Oscars of fashion. Winners of the competition as well as the finalists get great media exposure that increases their sales, thanks to being on the television show of the competition on Ovation TV."

—**Sandhya Garg**, fashion designer
and *Project Runway* participant

Internships

Along with a formal education, on-the-job training can be invaluable. If you study fashion design at an accredited school, you will probably have the chance to apply for an internship to get some real-world experience.

Interns are always overworked and underpaid. If you can live on little to no income and can manage long, crazy hours, the hard work could easily pay off with the industry contacts you'll make.

Professional Organizations

Another good way to develop industry contacts is to join professional organizations. They usually have local chapters where you can meet fashion design professionals and get to know them at networking events. Student memberships are available at discounted prices, and these organizations often have design school scholarships available to student members. Mentoring programs can match you up with a seasoned fashion industry insider. Even if there isn't a chapter in your area, you might still be able to participate virtually through discussion boards, online forums, and educational webinars.

❝You need to build a network of professionals and mentors you can trust and who can guide you. Designing is not something people do for money, it's something you do because you love to create and you love seeing people wear your creations.**❞**

— **Ani Hovhannisyan**, wardrobe stylist/editor

Some professional organizations for fashion design include:

- The Fashion Group International (**www.fgi.org**)

- The Council of Fashion Designers of America (**www.cfda.com**)

- The Costume Designers Guild (**www.costumedesignersguild .com**)

- The American Apparel and Footwear Association (**www.apparelandfootwear.org**)

- The International Apparel Federation (**www.iafnet.com**)

Working Your Way Up in the Business

Although Ralph Lauren didn't finish college, trying to break into the world of fashion without a degree may be the hardest way to go. However, Mr. Lauren proved it can be done. He worked as a tie salesman for Brooks Brothers before launching his own line.

"To be in the fashion industry in general, you need a lot of ambition and willpower. You need to be persistent, especially during the many failures of your career. There will be ups and downs, but you need to stay on track. I've noticed designers aren't just creatives—they are strategists, too. They are able to make decisions that will impact their company and drive sales. It's incredibly difficult to just be a creative right now; you have to have a business perspective.**"**

— **Ani Hovhannisyan**, wardrobe stylist/editor

If you want to follow in his footsteps, some entry-level positions in fashion design that may be open to someone with no experience include design assistant, junior visual merchandiser, and assistant buyer. A part-time job in a retail apparel store can get you started right now working toward these types of positions.

CASE STUDY: MOZIAH "MO" BRIDGES

I4-Year-Old Fashion Designer and Entrepreneur

Founder of Mo's Bows and Shark Tank Contestant

Mo's Story

I started my company when I was nine years old, and I started because I couldn't find any other bowties that really fit my style or my personality. So, that's when I asked my grandmother to teach me how to sew. From that point, I started an Etsy, and then, I would sell my bowties for bags of chips or trade them for rocks. We would go out to farmer's markets, and we would do local shows and local trunk shows. After that, I would make it into the newspaper, and then the newspaper contacted the magazine. And then the magazine went to the show, and then the show went from show to show to show to show. I didn't think it would get this big, but my hard work and dedication led me to this point.

Shark Tank actually called us and they wanted us to be on the show. Originally, my mom said no because she didn't want to have us crying on the show. We went out to LA, and we shot the show, but it wasn't for sure that we were actually going be on the show; it was just, like, a thing that we did. But then, when it got to that point, we were so excited that we got the opportunity.

If you didn't see the show, I didn't walk away with the check, but Daymond [John] did offer to be my mentor. He's just been guiding me through the practical aspects of owning my own company. He's taught me always to stay true to your company and never sell out your brand. Always know your brand, and just be yourself. My particular brand is fashionable with a touch of class, and urban.

[Mo's Bows bowties] are in a lot of stores. I have 12 to 15 stores that they're in right now, but, where I get most of the profit is from online, and that's my website at **mosbowsmemphis.com**. Someone helped me [make the website]. We have a whole Mo's Bows team that helps.

Advice for Teens Interested in Fashion

I would tell them to always figure out what you like doing and find out how you can make a profit out of it. And, also, just to be true to yourself and believe in yourself. I think believing in yourself means invest in yourself, and just stay true to your brand, like Daymond always taught me.

I do give back to the community. I have my Go Mo! Summer Camp Scholarship, and 100 percent of the proceeds help kids go to summer camp, because in Memphis it's hot, and childhood hunger is at its highest in the summertime because kids aren't eating that nutritious meal [that they're eating] when school time is in. So, I figured they can have fun, go to the movies, go to the swimming pool, and just be kids.

Future Goals

I want to be a fashion designer, and I want to have my own clothing line by the time I'm 20. I want to go to Parsons School of Design and hopefully get a Range Rover in the process of that.

Chapter Three

Developing Your Fashion Focus

If you've ever opened a fashion magazine, you know these truths:

Kate Spade = handbags
Steve Madden = shoes
Under Armour = performance wear

Most fashion designers end up focusing on one or two genres, and even the largest design houses do not try to cover every genre. Many online entrepreneurs find success with a narrow focus on a very specific niche.

Couture

The term *haute couture* technically can only be used by companies that meet specific standards in their garment construction and business operations, but "couture" has become synonymous with high fashion, custom-made formal wear. Couture designs often include unique architecture, lavish fabric, and hand-sewn detailing (think celebrities on the red carpet).

Lady Gaga at the 52nd Grammy Awards in Los Angeles, California.
Editorial Photo Credit: Joe Seer

Fast Fact

The term haute couture is of French origin and originated in the early 20th century. The expression translates to "high dressmaking" or "high fashion."

Outerwear

Outerwear just means coats, jackets, headwear, and all the accessories that people use to stay comfortable in any weather. Most people need outerwear for special occasions, sports, business, and travel. Outerwear design is a highly specialized field that requires not just creativity but some scientific knowledge about how fibers react to different humidity levels and temperatures. Outerwear designers also have to consider how fabrics move and layer over other clothing.

Wedding gowns

Although couture or formalwear designers may include a white dress or two in their seasonal collections, wedding gowns are an entirely separate specialty. Brides want to express themselves on their special day, and that often includes a one-of-a-kind dress.

Not all brides dream of a traditionally long, frilly poof of white satin and lace. You might set yourself apart from traditional collections by designing more creative wedding apparel that reflects the bride's ethnic, religious, or personal background. Don't forget about other specialties like plus size, petite, and mature brides.

Sports/performance apparel

In today's society, everyone, from elite professional athletes to occasional yoga class-goers, wants activewear that is high-performance and stylish. Many sports require clothing with practical features. Runners need shorts with seams that will not cause chafing. Mountain bikers need comfortable pants with padding where their legs hit the saddle. Alpine skiers need thin, warm layers they can remove quickly on the trail.

Did You Know?

Consumer demand is higher than ever for bicycling wear for larger men and women, called "Clydesdales" and "Athenas."

A related type of specialty clothing is dance apparel. Many forms of dance have traditional styles of clothing, but there is always room for improvement or innovation. Scottish dancers need highly embroidered skirts, but an inventive designer may be able to create the required look using moisture-wicking technical fabrics.

Petites

If you are 5'4" or under, you still want to be on fleek, and you know a lot of times the ensemble that looks good on a 5'11" model makes someone a foot shorter look dumpy and feel unattractive.

Designs for petite women should have different lines and cuts than patterns for taller clients. Short girls know that simply hemming pants and skirts doesn't work. Like people of any height, petites need casual clothing, sports apparel, formal wear, and business attire.

Plus size

If you are a curvy girl or a husky guy, you know that plus size women and men also need clothing that fits their bodies and their lifestyles. Larger-sized clothing may incorporate seaming that accentuates curves and minimizes bulkiness. A good plus-wear designer knows which fabrics add visual weight to clothing and should be avoided.

The newer Junior Plus division offers younger women the same stylish looks they see from popular brands like Wet Seal and Forever 21 in sizes larger than 13.

Did You Know?

More than half of American women wear size 14 or larger and are considered "plus size."

Children

Contemporary children's fashions can range from cut-down versions of adult styles to those fussy vintage looks grandparents love to buy. Parents like to dress their kids to reflect their lifestyle and values, so customers who purchase vegan, ethnic, or religious clothing for themselves want similar choices for their children.

Girls and boys involved in pageants, athletics, and dance need targeted clothing and accessories. Families may want a coordinated look for family photos. Just like adults, children come in many sizes. Age-appropriate clothing for plus size, slim, tall, and petite children can be difficult to find outside of bigger cities, and parents may look to online retailers.

Costumes and historical wear

Hollywood employs the largest number of costume designers, but there are opportunities even in small-town community theaters and schools. With the right marketing, you might even be able to find a niche creating inventive and unique Halloween costumes.

If you love the challenge of recreating historic looks that are perfect down to the smallest detail, you might also enjoy designing for historical re-enactors. Creating authentic costumes takes a lot of research, and customers who want them will gladly pay for quality pieces.

Men wearing historical costumes at the Esclade festival in the old city of Geneva.
Editorial Photo Credit: Nina Mikryukova

CASE STUDY: MAUREEN DEMERS, MFA

Costume Designer

Maureen (Molly) Demers "fell madly in love" with costume design while in college to earn her theater degree.

"It's exciting; it changes all the time," she says of her job in Ocala, Florida. "I like to build and create. I love historical replication."

Molly encourages students interested in costume design to consider a theater degree rather than focusing only on fashion design. "Try every area of theater," she says. "You will be more successful if you understand the other areas like acting, directing, set design and lighting. If you are well-rounded and knowledgeable, you understand what the actors and director need from you, and you can do your job more collaboratively with everyone else."

Molly recommends students get experience by volunteering with a school or community theater and says a young person can even learn a lot about fabrics and all the pieces involved by working at a fabric store.

Lifestyle wear

The term "lifestyle wear" is pretty generic, just meaning that people want fashion that supports their lifestyle and career choices. For vegans, this means not using any animal products like leather, fur, or wool. Environmentalists may look for clothes that are made with "green" materials and methods.

If you've ever had to wear a uniform, you know that many jobs require industry-specific apparel, not just for the look but for performance. It may not sound like a glamorous niche for a designer, but kitchen workers and

medical personnel need sturdy clothing that can weather repeated wash-
ings in hot water and feature plenty of pockets. Workers in construction
trades need clothes that move with them, keep them comfortable and safe
at various temperatures, and are in colors that don't show dust and dirt.
You can see that the list of lifestyle subsets is practically endless.

Special needs

If you've ever broken your arm or injured your hand, you know that but-
toning a shirt with one hand is impossible. People with special needs or
physical limitations need clothes adapted to their abilities. An older person
who's had a stroke may need special fasteners. Breastfeeding mothers need
blouses and dresses with the right access.

Creating adaptive clothing requires more than just fashion sense and technical ability. You might enjoy the challenge of resolving accessibility issues

without compromising your style vision, and you might find meeting the needs of special populations especially rewarding.

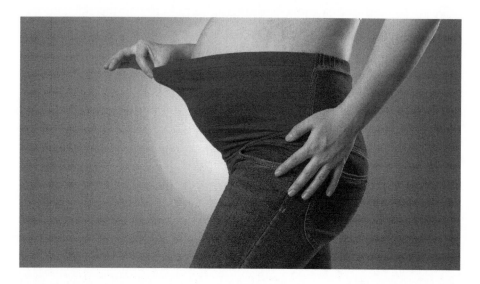

Menswear

Usually, men's fashion doesn't change as quickly or as remarkably as women's, but men also need a range of wardrobe choices that fit their lifestyles. Menswear designers might specialize in business attire, formal wear, wedding apparel, or athletic and performance wear.

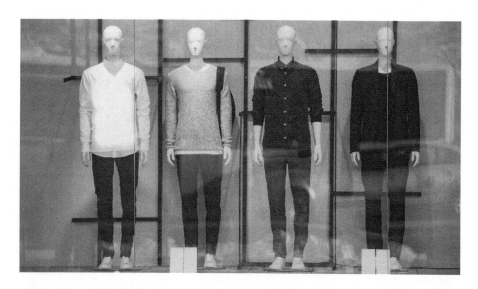

Accessories

Your client is not fully dressed until he or she is accessorized — it's a fashion rule. If you enjoy designing jewelry or accessories, you might focus entirely on an accessory line or present them in coordination with your clothing line.

There are as many categories of accessories as there are genres of clothing. Athletes need bags to carry their equipment and clothing to wear to the gym or track. Brides need veils, shoes, garters, and jewelry. Handbags and shoes need to be on point for the season, they need to be made from quality materials, and they must be functional. In an office, a distinctive briefcase makes a statement. Belts, wallets, socks, and smartphone cases are accessories that people use every day.

Finding Your Niche

In the crowded fashion design industry, it can be difficult for you to distinguish yourself as a new designer in one of the broad style categories. Unless you offer something different and exciting, potential customers are more likely to purchase from a more established company.

People enjoy dressing to reflect their personality and passions. You can find potential fashion design niches wherever special interests intersect with basic wardrobe needs. If you design and market outerwear, formal attire, accessories, sportswear, or business clothing that reaches any underserved market, the results can pay off. The secret is to find that market.

> **"**There's a lot that goes into finding your niche. Look at it from a business perspective: How many people specialize in this niche? What's the competition? What am I doing that's different than them? Is it corny or overdone? Speculate, and then make a decision. It's not something that may come right away. Sometimes, you need opinions from people who can give you different insights to your specific niche. This is where your mentors come in — ask the people you trust what their honest opinions are.**"**
>
> — **Ani Hovhannisyan**, wardrobe stylist/editor

One way to stand out with your designs is to look for overlapping niches with markets that are currently underserved. Snow sports such as skiing and tubing, for instance, require clothes that are insulated and rugged but are still thin enough to allow the athlete to move. There are many companies that produce stylish and high quality winter sports clothing, but a brand that sells vegan or vintage-inspired snow wear may find a whole new group of customers eager to buy their pieces.

> **"**The only way you can rise above the chaos and noise is to be laser focused and to find a niche that you can dominate.**"**
>
> — **Monil Kothari**, Founder of Antandre,
> a jewelry e-commerce company

OK, put your thinking cap on! Let's begin brainstorming about potential niches for your business by discovering your interests and experiences.

Your interests

Consider your interests, even those that don't seem directly related to fashion. Whether you enjoy volunteering with an environmental nonprofit organization, playing guitar with a local band, or walking your dog in the woods, the other people who like the same things you do are your potential clients. Because you share a hobby, you already have common ground to relate to them.

Your experiences

Now reflect on your experiences with your hobby, especially as they are related to clothing and accessories. If you often canvas your neighborhood with flyers for your favorite charity, you might want a vest with pockets just the right size to hold pamphlets. If you are a musician, you might dream of an ethnic-print gig bag. If you're a pet lover, you might enjoy a coat with the pocket slit for the leash so you can keep your hands warm while walking your dog.

Unmet needs

Google is your friend to research what fashion options are available to solve the problems you identified. Think of all the different types of people who might have the same problem, and determine what markets are underserved. You might find that there are designers who offer utility vests, for example, but only in conservative cuts and colors that would not appeal to younger, trendier customers.

How to Use the Niche Brainstorming Worksheet

Try using the following worksheet to help you organize ideas for finding your market niche.

To complete the worksheet, list your hobbies in the "Interests" circle. Then, list needs you have come across while pursuing your hobbies. Finally, list groups of people who also might have those needs in the "Potential Markets" circle.

For example, a designer who attends weekly yoga and tribal dance classes may notice that she is uncomfortably cold at the beginning of class. Other people seem to have the same problem, and several students wear pale pink leg warmers and shrugs they can slip off once their muscles are warmed up. The knitwear clashes with the earth tones of the yoga and dance clothing. When the designer talks to her classmates, she finds that the leg warmers and shrugs are from ballet clothing manufacturers.

The designer might use the information to create the following example worksheet, which helps her determine that there might be a market for leg warmers and shrugs crafted from organic fiber naturally dyed in earth tones, coordinated with the outfits she usually sees students wear to yoga and tribal dance classes.

Niche Brainstorming Worksheet

Interests

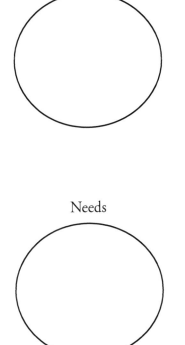

Potential Markets

Needs

Design Ideas

Niche Brainstorming Worksheet

Interests

Yoga
Tribal Dance

Potential Markets

Vegan
Petites
Men

Needs

Leg warmers and shrugs
(most are made for ballet
dancers and are pastel,
solid colors).

Design Ideas

Leg warmers and shrugs,
knit from organic cotton,
with Indian and African-
inspired patterns, with
extended sizes for petites
and men

Expanding your niche

Once you have determined a need and a potential market, it's a great idea to think bigger. The initial niche you define doesn't have to be your end target. Unless your dream is to design those particular articles, think of them as a stepping stone toward advancing your fashion business.

A designer who starts by creating accessories for tennis players, for example, may decide to expand into tennis outfits and training clothing after he or she gains name recognition within the market.

On the other hand, if you enjoy designing for the niche you have carved out for your business and find success in the market, there is nothing wrong with specializing in one particular product. Fashion is a dynamic, constantly changing industry, and there are ample opportunities to experiment with new techniques, patterns, and materials. Even designing within a narrow scope can remain challenging and fun.

"I started out producing wedding photo shoots for my friend's website, and I realized I love dressing people. I had a blog, so the connections to PR and showrooms were already there. All I had to do was ask. I asked photographers to work with me, and so many trusted me without experience. That's how I grew my book. I just asked people if they wanted to create with me, and I worked really hard once they said yes to the finished editorial. I went on to start my own magazine with an investor, and then later on helped a friend start hers. I started contributing to Zink Magazine and then shooting editorials for international magazines. This year, I launched my bridal styling business, Through The Veil, and I will be styling brides for their wedding day, engagement party, and bridal showers.**"**

— Ani Hovhannisyan, wardrobe stylist/editor

Finding Inspiration

After you decide on a niche for your business, you can start focusing your designs. One way to develop a cohesive line is to create apparel based on a common source of inspiration.

Once you're tuned into it, you can find inspiration anywhere and everywhere. Look for places, objects, or events that are rich in texture, color, shapes, or patterns. You may find the perfect piece in your environment; nature is full of potential sources. Your seasonal collection could draw from the palette of forest colors in autumn or the textural pattern of a snake's skin. You could base an entire line on the gentle curve and subtle color variations of a single daffodil petal. The environment also includes manmade elements. The lines of a skyscraper, the textures on a brick wall, and the colors on a mural might inspire you.

"Instagram is a huge treasure chest of inspiration.**"**

— **Ani Hovhannisyan**, wardrobe stylist/editor

You might find inspiration from past fashions, architecture, and technology. You could design clothes based on the practical women's separates from World War II or the light, feminine styles found a few years later. The clean, organic lines of prairie-style buildings might lend themselves to the silhouettes of your wedding dresses. You might find an antique lamp, table, or toy that calls to you. The delicate weathering and aged colors could provide a basis for your designs.

"I get a lot of inspiration from furniture. Furniture lines and clothing lines sync.**"**

— **Molly Demers**, costume designer

Textiles from other cultures are common sources of design inspiration. You can pull a single motif or a selection of colors from a woven blanket to use as a unifying element in your line. You can gather spices, fibers, photographs, and artwork from a single location and look for common colors, textures, and patterns to sprinkle throughout your pieces.

You may draw your inspiration from current trends, but keep in mind that the pieces you design today may not be seen in stores for another year or 18 months. By then, your looks may seem outdated. Instead of looking at your local department and specialty stores for inspiration, check out how people are modifying their clothing—are trendy guys and girls rolling up their sleeves, cutting off their jeans, or replacing their shirt buttons with safety pins? Pay special attention to groups that seem to be a trend or two ahead of your target market.

Did You Know?

Some 6,000 design companies and retailers around the world subscribe to the World Global Style Network (WGSN), which predicts trends two years in advance. They watch both top-down, or "catwalk" fashion trends, which come from fashion houses and runways, and bottom-up, or "sidewalk" fashion trends seen on the street. Right now, their biggest influence in sidewalk fashion is Generation Z, born after the year 2000.[5]

How to Create a Storyboard

Designers use storyboards to show the elements that inspire a certain line. Your storyboard is really just a collage to help you organize these elements, see new connections between them, and present them to other people.

The first step toward creating a storyboard is to gather items that represent your inspiration. If your designs will be based around a piece of cloth, photograph, or small item, this is a straightforward step. However, if your inspiration is less tangible—for example, a sun setting over a mountain range—you may need to be more creative in what you include. You may want to collect a picture of your inspiration or even several pictures from different angles.

"Sometimes ... you have to focus on something simple, like a flower petal or the shapes on the street as the sun is coming down.**"**

—Ani Hovhannisyan, wardrobe stylist/editor

---

5. Trufelman, 2016

Now, collect other materials that support your inspiration. Make sample swatches using paints, fabrics, or fibers that capture the colors of your inspirational moment. Be sure to make several samples of each so you can play with how the elements interact together. Sketch out a few rough silhouettes based on the lines of your source. Look for other objects that echo any textural components. Find anything that reminds you of your inspiration in some way.

For example, if a morning at the beach was your inspiration, you might collect fabric swatches in the colors of the ocean, photos of the sunrise, and shells you picked up out of the sand. Your sketches might echo the flow of the water or lines represented by the shapes of the shells.

Once you have gathered plenty of swatches, images, and objects, it's time to play! Lay all the materials on your worktable, and start making connections. Give yourself plenty of time to see what works together and what should be weeded out, but just because something is not directly connected to your inspiration doesn't mean you shouldn't include it. Some pieces might be in a progression from your inspiration.

For example, if your line will be built around an heirloom quilt with a gray background, you might find some pebbles that are the same shade of gray. The texture of the pebbles might connect a series of fabrics and colors not found on the original inspiration piece.

File away any materials not connected to your original inspiration or that do not work together with the other elements, but don't throw them away! If you liked the pieces enough to collect them, you might decide they do belong on your storyboard later, or you may want to use them for another collection.

When you have decided what you will include on your storyboard, find a suitable mounting board and start working with different arrangements and layouts. Mounting boards come in a variety of sizes, colors, and materials. When choosing a mounting board, keep in mind where you plan to take your storyboard, how you will display it, and the number, colors, sizes, and weights of the elements it is to hold. Mounting boards made by sandwiching a thick foam core between two sheets of paper are often a good choice as they are sturdy and easy to cut and drill. You can display a foam board by leaning it against a wall or by setting it up on an easel.

Storyboard layouts

Once you have selected the elements you are displaying, it is time to organize the components to tell the inspiration story of your line or design.

The layout you choose depends on the type and number of elements you include. If you have one large inspiration piece and many supporting swatches, you can mount the inspiration piece near the center of the board and circle swatches around it. In an outer circle, arrange pieces that have a secondary relationship to the inspiration piece. To create a cohesive storyboard, place secondary swatches near the element that ties them to the inspiration piece.

If you have several connected inspiration pieces, mount them on the board with connecting swatches creating a flow between the inspiration pieces.

If you have a single inspiration piece with only a few supporting swatches or if you are presenting a completed design, consider a clean layout with the inspiration piece or final drawing on one side and supporting swatches on the other.

If you drew your ideas from many elements instead of a central inspiration, a freeform collage might be the most complete way to represent your line.

As you experiment with different layouts and move the materials around, you might want to use temporary adhesive putty to keep each element in position.

Once you are super-sure of your layout and the position of each element, you can permanently attach the pieces to the storyboard. Some mounting boards are self-adhesive; others need glue. Before you use any adhesive, test it on a small piece of the swatch, picture, or object to make sure the glue doesn't cause any damage or discoloration. You may need several varieties of glue for a single storyboard.

How to Use a Storyboard

If you constructed a storyboard to show the inspiration behind a work in progress, keep the board where you can see it and refer to it whenever you work on the line or design. Take it with you to suppliers to make sure any fabric, fiber, trim, or accessories you purchase are the right colors and textures. Do not trust your memory! Hold swatches up to your storyboard to make sure they are compatible with the inspirational elements.

Be aware that colors and patterns can appear differently under natural versus artificial light. In dim warehouses or storage areas, it can be hard to tell what coordinates and what clashes. Do not be afraid to ask to take a bolt of cloth outside to compare it to the samples on your storyboard. Or carry a small flashlight with you so you can analyze supplies on the spot.

Never assume that all units grouped together on a shelf or in a bin are the same color. Even subtle color mistakes can stand out on and detract from a finished garment. Check and double-check every component before you buy it. Keep your receipts in case you need to return items because of color imperfections.

If you are using the storyboard to present a design or line to clients, take extra care to keep it pristine. To limit damage from moving or storing the board, attach a protective cover that can be removed or flipped to the back so that potential customers can touch swatches and evaluate textures. Consider making a separate, portable storyboard to take with you on shopping trips or to use in the workroom.

CASE STUDY: DEANNA KEI

Designer, Stylist, and Fashion
Illustrator

www.deannakei.com
Instagram: @deannakei

Great collections often begin with a concept board. Pull inspiration from everywhere you can think of! Magazine clippings, photographs, flower petals—anything that speaks to you. You can also look to the runway shows for trends. It's helpful to organize all your musings into a collage. You can create it digitally or the old-fashioned way. The purpose of your board is to help you organize your ideas and decide on a direction for your designs. This is also called a mood board.

The inspirational images in this mood board have been slightly blurred for copyright reasons. The idea is that you can piece together clippings of other people's work for your own inspiration. Hopefully, this rendering still helps you to see how colors and textures can come together to create a mood.

The next step is to select your color palette and fabrics. You can pull colors from your mood board, let your fabrics determine your colors, or choose whatever you like. Finalizing a palette helps you to keep the fabrics for the collection cohesive.

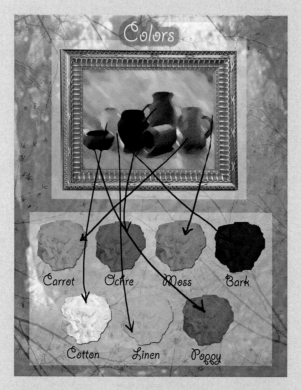

Now, you're ready to start sketching! No two designers have the same sketching style. Yours can be as polished or as rough as you want. Look to your fabrics and mood board for inspiration.

Sketches from The International Fashionista's Lookbook Diary.

These small pre-sketches are called thumbnails. This is your spot to brainstorm and really get creative. You'll separate the good from the bad later, so don't worry about that.

After you choose your favorite sketches, it's time to put them on figures! Think about where to place seams and closures like zippers or buttons. Look at your own clothing to see how it's constructed. Lay all your figures out together. How do they look? Do the outfits fit together as a solid collection? You may decide to add or remove pieces or mix them up. Once you finalize where to use your colors and fabrics, you're ready to start rendering! (Coloring in a fashion figure is called rendering.)

You can combine a variety of mediums and techniques to achieve your desired look. Try experimenting with different tools.

These figures are digitally rendered in Photoshop.

After you've got your outfits filled in, it's time to work on the layout. It's important to consider color, silhouette, and even the model's pose when placing your figures. What looks good together? Which outfits complement each other?

Now you're ready for the finishing touches. You can choose to set your figures on any kind of mount or board you like. Remember to tie it into the rest of your pages.

There's so much more to creating a cohesive presentation than having pretty designs. You want your final presentation to be the best representation of your work — and if you put your heart into each step, it will be!

Chapter Four

Designing Your Line

Design Basics

Becoming a good designer will take study, practice, and experimentation. You need to look at your work and the work of other designers with a critical eye. You may need to sketch dozens of ideas before you find a look you like enough to develop. Experiment with creativity — don't be afraid to try new ideas or arrange traditional concepts in fresh ways. This is where your youth and inexperience will work to your advantage.

Before you can break the rules, you need to understand them. Fashion design has 11 general principles:

1. Line

2. Form

3. Rhythm

4. Balance

5. Proportion

6. Focal point

7. Color

8. Texture

9. Hand

10. Unity

11. Contrast

Consider each principle by itself and as part of the entire garment when editing your designs.

Line

Line refers to the silhouette of a design. If you are evaluating the line of an existing garment, you should consider how it would look in two dimensions and trace the outside edges created by the fabric. You can actually reduce even complex fashion to a simple geometric shape like a triangle, oval, or rectangle, or a combination of two or three shapes. When someone wears a garment, his or her body, in addition to the cut and seaming, may influence the line of material. If you want a garment with a rigid line, as opposed to a flow that follows the model's curves, you need to use a very firm fabric or use structural components like padding or boning.

> **"**A beautiful dress may look beautiful on a hanger, but that means nothing. It must be seen on the shoulders, with the movement of the arms, the legs, and the waist.**"**
>
> **— Coco Chanel**, iconic French fashion designer

Form

The line creates the form of the garment. If line is two-dimensional, then form is how much space the design occupies in three dimensions. The form of a piece of clothing can be hard to describe with a single sketch, so designers may draw the garment from several angles. This is especially important if the garment has complicated form elements, such as bellows or ruffles.

Rhythm

The pattern of the fabric you choose and the placement of details across the garment help guide the viewer's eye. For example, thick diagonal stripes that begin at the shoulders and converge at the waist draw attention to the midline. The way people look across a piece, where their eyes linger, and what parts they skip, create the rhythm of the outfit.

Balance

How the patterns, graphics, details, and trim are positioned on the garment also help determine the visual weight of the design. Balance describes how evenly the visual weight is distributed. Most fashion designs are balanced from left to right, but the two sides don't have to be perfectly symmetrical. Different elements can provide similar visual weight and can balance each other. Consider an asymmetric sleeveless shirt that is designed to be worn off the shoulder on one side. A lower or detailed hem on the same side as the bare shoulder could provide enough visual weight to make the design balanced and attractive.

Depending on the style, balance from top to bottom can be even or uneven. Evenly-balanced designs have the same visual weight above the waist as they do below. This can be achieved by using the same patterns in the same proportions. An evenly balanced design can be achieved by using smaller amounts of more vivid elements—like a leopard-print blouse with a neutral skirt.

Proportion

Balance is closely related to proportion. Where balance refers to the visual weight of a garment, proportion refers to the relative size of the component pieces. Small and large pieces can be combined for very effective designs; for example, a voluminous skirt paired with a fitted shirt.

Focal point

Embroidery at the neckline of a blouse, a wild graphic on a casual T-shirt, and industrial-inspired buckles on a formal pump are all details that catch the viewer's attention and encourage them to look longer. These details are the focal points of the garments—the element that is emphasized. You can create a focal point with cut, seams, trim, graphics, or other elements. Keep in mind that a focal point is a single design feature.

Color

When selecting a color scheme for your design, consider both the tone and the value of your options. Colors right next to each other influence each other, so be sure to experiment with swatches before committing to any fabric or trim. A book or course in color theory can help you learn how to use the color wheel to develop effective color combinations.

Texture

Texture refers to the surface quality of the garment. The texture of a fabric is the result of the fibers used to create the fabric and the technique used to weave or knit it. A subtle texture may not be obvious to viewers unless they are very close, but the right texture can be the difference between a design that works and one that won't catch a buyer's eye. Textures can be difficult to show on a sketch, so consider attaching a swatch of fabric if the texture is an important feature in your design.

Hand

Clothing can be stiff and rigid, like a leather jacket, or flexible and fluid, like a silk dress. The hand of a garment is a description of how it drapes and flows when touched. Hand is more than texture; it includes the weight and thickness of the fabric, the fibers used, and the tightness of the weave. The hand of the fabric you choose will help determine how the garment hangs and how seams and trimmings sit.

Unity

The unity of a design refers to the connection between the different pieces of the garment. One way to create unity in your design is through repetition. Nearly any design element can be repeated — you can use the same line or form in a shirt as in a skirt. You can repeat patterns, textures, and colors throughout a piece. Unity helps create a sense that the design is intentional.

Contrast

Contrasting colors, textures, proportions, lines, forms, and hands add interest to your design. A slice of white on a black skirt can be a focal point, or it can be a unifying element between the skirt and a white blouse. The more different the elements are, the more intensely they contrast. A blue stripe at the hem of a turquoise shirt can leave the viewer wondering if there had been a piecing or dyeing mistake. The same blue stripe on a red shirt gives an obvious contrasting effect.

CASE STUDIES: DREAMGIRL INTERNATIONAL

Dreamgirl International is an award-winning lingerie company based in California. The head designers, Lisa Dixon and Julie Hunot, give their advice on how to develop your fashion focus, how to get inspired, and how to make your passion a reality.

Designer: Lisa Dixon
Title: Design Director

Finding Your Niche

In my opinion, in order to really "find your niche," you must make an effort to expose yourself to as many different genres as possible. My first design job right out of school was as an assistant designer for a children's swimwear manufacturer. I liked it; it was creative and fun, but I didn't quite feel that children's wear was my passion or my strength. (Although at that time I didn't really know where my strength and passion rested yet.) My next job was designing lingerie. I definitely liked it better, but at that time, I still wasn't sure that "this was it."

The next decade or so, I moved around the country and changed jobs every couple of years so I was able to gain experience designing in many other categories, including menswear (dress shirts as well as casual attire), golf wear, sweaters and ladies' contemporary swimwear, and classic women's swimwear. By the time I worked my way up from an assistant designer to a design director, I finally figured out that I had a passion for women's contemporary swimwear as well as lingerie (which are a very similar skill set). In my current position, I am responsible for designing and merchandising a ladies' lingerie line, and this is probably the most fun I've ever had in my career. (When you are spending so much time at a job, it's fabulous if it can be fun, too!)

Finding Inspiration

For me, inspiration comes at different times and different places ... or sometimes not at all. I have found inspiration from a variety of sources—on the runways, shopping, traveling, in my dreams, people-watching, social media—anywhere, really. However, there are also times that I can look all around and find absolutely none! In those times, I sometimes need to stop and do something else. I have to clear my head of fashion and read world news, current events, or something completely different. Then, it comes back when I least expect it. I have actually woken up in the middle of the night with ideas, so I always keep a sketchpad and pencil close to my bed.

I also have found inspiration from one genre and applied it to another with great success. For example, when I was designing women's swimwear, I got a lot of inspiration from looking at designer evening gowns, the way something drapes, different back treatment concepts, jewelry details, etc. Fashion and trends change so quickly; it's important to keep an open mind and look outside of just your genre of design—or even fashion as a whole—to gain new inspiration.

Designer: Julie Hunot
Title: V.P. of Lingerie Product Development & Design

Finding Your Niche

My suggestion to anyone starting out in the fashion industry is to take a job at a small company vs. working at a name-brand place. Yes; working at a very well-known company may seem really impressive, but you will never get a good understanding of the business as a whole by starting out at such a large company. When you work for a small company, you will have the opportunity to learn so many more skills and gain invaluable experience.

Another reason I personally value working at a smaller company is the diversity of creativity you are allowed. In most large companies, you work in a very specific department; for example, "woven tops." Once you're in that department, you will literally ONLY work on woven tops, and you generally aren't able to even give another department an idea you might have. However; when you are working for a smaller company, you are able to gain experience in all departments, not just one segment. You are really able to create a full collection based on your vision.

Finding Inspiration

Timing is an important consideration when finding your inspiration. You really need to "read" the flow of the industry you are in. It's always important to be on-trend and keeping up with what's new, but some genres take more time to filter down. For example, in the lingerie industry, I have found that a design theme or trend will not be popular — or accepted by the consumer — until about one year after it hits the runways. If you come out with a very fashionable item at the wrong time for your industry, it will just sit on the shelf and will eventually become sale merchandise. But if you can read and understand the flow of your specific market, then you will be able to come out with the right product at the right time.

Another way I find inspiration is to watch how people style themselves as well as how companies style their product in catalogs. For example, in the hosiery industry, companies would style the fishnet pantyhose with a cute boy short over them, so the imagery isn't too risqué. This led to a new idea for the industry: Why not design pantyhose with the built-in boy short look? Now, this style has become a standard in everyone's line.

Designing Your Line

Some words of wisdom when fine-tuning your final design: Make sure the final product is also approachable for the end consumer who might not be as "up" on all of the fashion trends as you and others in the industry are. For example, if you create a new and unique trend idea, offer it in a basic color; don't also do that design in a new fashion color. Don't make the consumer work too hard to accept the new concept.

Sketching Your Ideas

Almost all fashion designers edit and rework their ideas, because making the design elements work together can be a complicated process. Drawing can help you see how different components work together, and you can try out new looks. If you create custom fashions for your clients, a quick sketch can help you communicate your vision and clarify what the customer wants.

❝We have a rendering for everything. We have to create and build and show drawings to the director. It's a collaboration.**❞**

— **Molly Demers**, costume designer

Most traditional fashion design education programs teach figure drawing in addition to garment construction and design. If you learn the basics of how to draw the human body, you will better understand anatomy and proportion, and you can produce professional-looking fashion drawings to promote your designs in marketing publications and web pages.

If you already know how to draw figures, you will see that fashion drawings have a different proportion than realistic drawings. In nature, the length of an average human body is seven and one half times the length of the head. In fashion drawings, this proportion is increased to eight and a half, which presents a longer leg and helps show fashions to their best advantage.

There are three main types of fashion drawings:

1. Working drawings are used to show the details of a garment's construction to the pattern cutter.

2. Quick poses are used to show ideas to clients or collaborators.

3. Finished drawings are used for presentations or publications. They show the style, line, and texture of the outfit and should be consistent with the designer company's image.

You can start practice sketching by copying fashion photographs. That will help you learn some common modeling poses and typical fabric movement. Until you are proficient at sketching, use a template to trace a figure when you need to experiment with different fashion ideas.

CASE STUDY: ERMELINDA MANOS

Las Vegas Fashion Designer

www.ermelindamanos.com
Instagram: @ermelindamdesigns

My inspiration when creating a collection comes from films, traveling, and fabric sourcing.

My designs are effortless and timeless. I like to accentuate the female form, as I design for a confident and elegant woman.

First, I start off by making mood boards, with inspirational images that help me keep focused on the style I want to design. This is helpful to maintain a cohesive collection. Elements, styles, and colors within the collection should be cohesive and all effortlessly flow together, or be able to mix and match the looks with each other. I start sketching my ideas out on my sketchbook, and I sketch the entire inspiration based on how I envision the model on the runway — from hair, makeup, shoes, and accessories to go with the design. After I make several sketches, I make a list of the elements that stand out the most and the fabrics I want to use. I always do a color and trend forecast to make sure that the colors I pick are in season. One of my favorite parts of designing is going to the garment district to source the fabrics, trims, the beading, and all of the materials needed for each design. Sometimes, the design is created after I find the fabric that inspires me.

Next, I lay out all of the fabrics and the materials as I play around with them and create more sketches. This allows me to have a clear vision of what each design will be, as I narrow down my sketches to six to 12 looks that would be the final looks created for the collection.

The production begins, and I always have music playing in the background as we start creating the samples. All of the patterns are either draped or drafted, but I prefer draped a lot more. I'm very hands on with the sample processes as it is the most crucial part of the design; there's room for adjustments during sampling that you cannot do once it's finalized. I love to sew by hand, more than sewing on the machine, which is why you will find my designs have a lot of details that are handmade. Usually, our fit model is always a standard size when we try on the designs to ensure they are wearable and fit correctly for the ideal woman we have in mind—and that the design is flawless. Once the sampling and fit is approved, we then produce the final look or make multiples of the design.

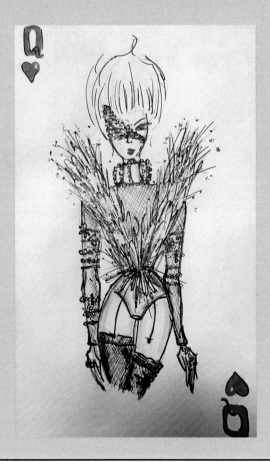

Hand sewing and creating dresses has been my first love since I was a child. I'm fortunate to be able to live out my childhood dream, but the fashion industry isn't always so glamorous. I spend many hours in the studio sewing, sampling, or running around downtown for endless hours to find the right bead or the right zipper. It's a fast-paced industry, and there's not a lot of time to sit and daydream when creating. Sometimes I have deadlines to create a design within hours, which is a lot of pressure. The results are very rewarding—the moment you see the gown draped on a woman's body, and the woman feeling confident and beautiful in my design. To be able to have my designs be part of women's lives, to be a reason for them to feel beautiful and smile, that is what makes everything worth it.

Selecting Materials

Before you get too far along in the design process, figure out what type of material you plan to use. Understanding the properties of the materials will help you make a realistic sketch.

Of course, several types of fibers and styles of fabric will often work with a single design. Cost may not matter in one-of-a-kind couture, but if you're designing an entire line, you may need to find similar fabrics that make your pieces affordable without changing the pattern and manufacturing process.

"One can write a whole series of books on types of fabrics and still leave out many options. Thanks to technology and innovation, great advances have been made in the field of fibers and fabrics. The best advice I can give any fashion designer is that it is very important to have a good knowledge of various fabrics, their properties, drape, and what fabric would work the best for which look. Fabrics are the foundation to any garment."

—**Sandhya Garg**, fashion designer
and *Project Runway* participant

Types of Fibers

There are two major categories of fibers: manmade and natural.

Manmade fibers can be made of cellulose or petroleum. Rayon is a cellulose-based fiber. Nylon is a petroleum product. Petroleum-based fibers are also called synthetic fibers. Manmade fibers have become popular in sports and performance wear since they can be engineered to wick moisture and keep the wearer drier and cooler in hot conditions.

Natural fibers can come from animals or plants. Animal fibers such as wool, mohair, and alpaca are good insulators, because the lofty filaments do not pack against each other. Plant fibers like hemp and cotton tend to absorb large amounts of water, making them good choices for warm-weather clothing. Natural fibers can be treated to change their original properties, like treating wool so it doesn't felt when washed in warm water.

Fast Fact

The term "felt" describes what happens to animal fibers when they mat together, changing the texture of the garment. This happens when the fiber gets warm and damp, like when your feet sweat inside a pair of wool socks.

Natural and manmade fibers can be used together to create blended fibers that combine the characteristics of their components. You know that adding a small amount of spandex to cotton gives some elasticity to the brittle natural fiber (think about your favorite pair of jeans). Garments made from blended fabric tend to keep their shape better than those made from pure linen, but they still have the look and feel of natural fibers.

Commonly used fibers

Once you have a design in mind, choose the right fiber to make it work. A dress that looks beautiful in a fluid, draping silk might not work with a stiff cotton. A pair of structured trousers, on the other hand, might look better with crisp linen. Even within the same fiber family, different types of spinning, weaving, or knitting produce fabric with different properties.

Check out the properties of some of the most popular fiber families:

Properties of Common Fibers						
Fiber	Water Management	Insulating	Softness	Wrinkling	Drape	Strength
Cotton	Absorbent	No	Soft	Heavy	Poor Drape	Strong
Linen	Absorbent	No	Soft	Heavy	Fair Drape	Strong
Ramie	Absorbent	No	Soft	Heavy	Fair Drape	Strong
Silk	Absorbent	Yes	Soft	Heavy	Good Drape	Strong
Wool	Absorbent	Yes	Depends on weave	Depends on weave	Good Drape	Weak
Acetate	Not absorbent	No	Soft	Light	Good Drape	Weak
Nylon	Not absorbent	No	Depends on weave	Light	Depends on weave	Strong
Acrylic	Absorbent	Yes	Soft	Light	Depends on weave	Strong
Polyester	Not absorbent	Yes	Depends on weave	Light	Depends on weave	Strong
Rayon	Absorbent	No	Soft	Heavy	Good Drape	Strong

Common natural fabrics

The same fibers can be woven or knit to create very different fabrics, which differ in appearance, care requirements, durability, drape, and texture. Here's how fabrics are classified according to fiber families.

Silk

Silk fiber is harvested from silkworm cocoons. Some common silk fabrics include:

- China silk: Plain weave, smooth silk fabric with a high luster

- Dupioni: Fabric woven from uneven silk threads

- Faille: Glossy, ribbed silk

- Georgette: Crinkled, sheer crepe

- Matelassé: Silk fibers woven with raised designs

- Noil: A soft fabric made of short silk fibers

- Organza: Thin, transparent silk

- Peau de Soie or paduasoy: Crisp fabric with thin cross ribs and corded appearance

- Pongee: A thin silk with a rough texture

- Silk linen: Plain weave silk with nubby crosshatches in both directions

Linen

Linen is woven from flax fiber, which is exceptionally strong and absorbent. The most common linen fabrics are:

- Butcher's linen: A heavy, canvas-like weave

- Damask: Plain or satin weave linen with a raised pattern

- Venise: Damask linen featuring a floral pattern and made out of very fine threads

Cotton

Cotton is a popular fiber because of its versatility. Cotton can be woven or knit by itself or blended with other fibers and is often used in casual life-style wear. The most common cotton fabrics include:

- Duck: Tightly woven canvas

- Muslin: Plain weave cotton of any thickness

- Organdy: Thin, transparent weave

- Poplin: Woven cotton with a small side-to-side rib

- Sateen: Satin weave cotton

- Terry cloth: Heavily piled, very absorbent cotton

Animal Fibers

Animal fiber is just animal hair—usually from sheep, alpacas, or camels. The fibers can be woven, knit, or even pressed numerous ways. Animal fibers include:

- Broadcloth: Woven fabric in a slight nap

- Challis: Light fabric woven to include a floral design

- Donegal: Woven tweed with thick slubs

- Felt: Compressed mat of fibers

- Flannel: Lightweight weave with a moderate nap

- Gabardine: Tightly woven twill

- Jersey: Lightweight knit of fine fibers

- Mackinaw: Heavy fabric with reversible, colored pattern

- Oatmeal cloth: Soft weave with a bumpy texture

- Tartan: Woven plaid

- Tweed: Thick, rough weave

Common manmade fabrics

"Technical" or "performance" fibers and fabrics are created from synthetic fibers or natural/synthetic fiber blends. These fabrics may be knit or woven to bring out specific qualities, usually related to how the fiber manages heat or water. Coolmax® from INVISTA is a family of technical fabrics that wick away perspiration and help wearers feel cool even in hot weather. Other technical fibers have increased insulating or water-repelling properties.

Like Coolmax®, most performance fibers and fabrics are trademarked products. LYCRA®, a registered trademark of INVISTA, for example, is a kind of spandex developed by DuPont. Brand-name fibers are more expensive than their parent fibers, because chemical companies invest a lot of time and money to develop and market technical fabrics.

To protect their image, the trademark holder may have strict guidelines for the use of the branded fiber, fabric, logo, motto, or name. If you decide to use a brand-name technical fabric, expect some limits on how creative you can be with your designs.

How to Identify Fibers

Especially while you're learning, an unlabeled fabric remnant from the bargain bin can be perfect for you to use to construct a test garment. Selling a garment is a different story.

Because of Federal Trade Commission labeling regulations, you may not be able to sell garments unless you are sure of the kind of fiber and its source. Being able to identify fabrics yourself can save you money and time.

The burn test isn't perfect, but it's a starting point to identify mystery fabrics, and the only tool you need is a match or lighter. (Note: yes, you can try this at home, but please have a fire extinguisher nearby. You'll be working with fire.)

The burn test can help you distinguish basics like whether a fabric is an animal, plant, or manmade fiber. It isn't really a good way to distinguish between different animal fibers like wool and alpaca, or between different plant fibers like hemp and cotton. Fabric blends are even tougher to identify.

If you like doing experiments (and playing with fire), grab the following worksheet, a fire extinguisher, and some fabric scraps!

Fiber Identification Worksheet

Note: Be sure to have a fire extinguisher handy when performing these tests.

1. Cut a small sample of the fiber. Using a pair of tweezers, hold the sample over a bowl of water. Light a long match or lighter, and bring the flame to the edge of the fiber sample.

If you see:	The fabric might be:
The fiber flames and burns quickly	Acrylic, acetate, or plant fibers (flax, cotton, or hemp)
The fiber burns slowly	Polyester or olefin
The fiber melts away from the flame and continues to burn slowly	Silk or animal fibers (wool, cashmere, or alpaca)

2. Remove the fiber from the flame.

If you see:	The fabric might be:
The fiber extinguishes but continues to melt	Acrylic, olefin, nylon, or polyester
The fiber burns and melts	Acetate
The fiber extinguishes	Silk or animal fibers (wool, cashmere, or alpaca)
The fiber glows	Plant fibers

3. Which best describes the ashes from the burnt fiber?

If the fibers look:	The fabric might be:
Hard and black	Acetate, acrylic, or polyester
Hard and gray	Nylon
Hard and brown	Olefin
Soft and black	Animal fibers, silk, or mercerized cotton
Soft and gray	Cotton, hemp, jute, or linen

Chapter Five

Sample Garments

Your design is perfected, and you've chosen your fabrics. Now you're ready to construct your first sample.

Sample garments have an important role in the fashion industry—they allow you to see your design on a model. Once you see the garment moving in three dimensions, you can figure out what it needs. The process of making the sample garment will also help you estimate the expense of producing that design. If you're going to manufacture a line for retail or wholesale, a bulk order reduces the cost per piece by as much as half of the sample cost.

Once you have completed sample garments, you're going to use them a lot. You can show them to buyers at fashion marts, trunk shows, or in-store demonstrations. Get a friend who's good with photography to take pictures of your samples to show your line in your portfolio and on your website. This is how you build your image.

Patternmaking

To construct your sample, you need a pattern to use to cut the material. If you get good at patternmaking, drafting your own patterns can save you a lot of time and money. If you have to hire a patternmaker, you might lose time by having to redo the pattern if he or she didn't understand your design and made a mistake. You also have to work around the patternmaker's schedule, which can leave you waiting weeks or even months for the completed patterns.

If you can draft your own patterns, that gives you another opportunity to fix problems or edit a look before the sample garments are constructed. If you don't have the technical skills to draft your own patterns, consider taking a course in patternmaking or draping. Until you are proficient, hire a professional.

If you hire a patternmaker, confirm that they have time for your project. Be sure to get an estimate for the cost. Some patternmakers charge by the hour, others charge by the piece. Get their deposit and editing policy in writing.

Patternmakers may specialize in certain types of garments. Choose one who has experience making the kind of clothing you design. The patternmaker will need to know everything about the look, including the widths and lengths of the components (including pockets and sleeves), detailing, and the fabric you plan to use. Your designs are your creative property. The patternmaker you choose should have a privacy policy to protect your work.

Basic Construction Skills

If you can sew well enough, you can also save money by constructing your own samples. Just remember that your samples are the buyers' first impression of you, so if you can't do a professional job, hire a contractor who will make your clothes look as good as possible.

If you design custom items, you may find it faster and easier to do your own sewing. Even if you intend to hire a seamstress or tailor, you can communicate with them much better if you understand sewing basics. You also want to be able to recognize poor work.

To understand construction basics, you need to be able to:

- Tell the difference between common types of seams
- Understand what seams work better for different fabrics, garments, and looks
- Set sleeves
- Understand the function and placement of facings, interfacings, and linings
- Insert zippers, snaps, and buttons
- Fit collars, lapels, and pockets
- Hem edges

If you're not already an expert sewer, you might find an affordable class at a local design school, craft store, or sewing machine dealer. Seamstresses and tailors sometimes offer private lessons.

"Take sewing classes. Know your way around an iron. Understand patterns, and practice as many as possible.**"**

—Molly Demers, costume designer

Sewing Equipment

If you don't plan to sew your own samples or garments, you may use a home sewing machine for experimentation and alterations. Home machines, even if they are labeled "semi-industrial" or "industrial strength," have substantially less power and sew much more slowly than industrial machines. They also tend to sew less consistent stitches, but they are much more affordable. You might find a good used sewing machine at a thrift shop or on Craigslist.

Once you are manufacturing clothes, you'll want to understand different types of industrial sewing machines and how they're used. Industrial sewing machines include:

Drop feed	Sews a straight stitch through lightweight to medium-weight fabrics
Needle feed	Sews a straight stitch through heavier fabrics
Walking foot	Sews a straight stitch through very thick or heavy fabrics
Zig zag	Allows for side-to-side motion in addition to straight stitch
Blind stitch	Makes a stitch that cannot be seen on the right side of the fabric (used for linings and cuffs)
Serger or overlock	Creates finished, trimmed seams

Hiring a Seamstress or Tailor

Until you have the skills and equipment, hiring someone to construct your samples may actually be less expensive than trying to do it yourself. Depending on your designs, your location, the number of samples you need, and how long you can wait, you may decide to have your samples sewn by a freelance sewer or by a clothing factory.

When interviewing people to sew your samples, keep in mind the following questions:

- Do they have the skills needed to complete the job, such as working with special fabrics?

- Do they have experience making that type of garment?

- Do they understand the special techniques required to construct the garment?

- What training have they received?

- Will they adjust the garment if it isn't right?

- Do they have the equipment needed to make the garment look perfect?

- How long will it take for them to complete the garment?

Take time to listen to sewers' input on construction techniques. They have experience and can help you figure out which hems, seams, and fasteners work with your chosen fabrics and cuts. They may offer helpful suggestions for better ways to get the same effects.

Just don't put professional sewers in the position of being the designer. They will not get any credit if an idea works, and it's not fair to blame them if their suggestion ruins a look.

Be sure to get several estimates before committing to a sewing contractor. Although the cheapest option is not always the best, talking with several sewers will help you understand more about the industry and the going rate of the service.

Keep in mind that contractors may be limited by the material you give them to work with. Check for damage and inconsistencies before you leave supplies with the sewer. Have them inspect the materials, too, and sign an inspection sheet noting any problems.

Signs of a High-Quality Garment

Before you accept a completed sample garment from a contractor, look it over carefully to make sure that it's sewn and fitted correctly.

What are you looking for?

Seams should lay smooth and have even stitching. Fasteners like zippers and buttons should be secure. The fabric grain-line of each part of the garment should match what was indicated in the pattern. Buttonholes should be neat and finished. If the garment is made from patterned fabric, the pattern should match up across the parts of the garment and be centered appropriately on the front. Hemlines should be even and clean. Check to make sure the material has not been damaged by pressing and that loose threads are trimmed.

If there are any metal or plastic details on the piece, make sure they are securely attached and free of burrs. There should not be any visible glue residue. Leather pieces should be of even thickness and finish. Trim should be sewn neatly and evenly, with smooth overlaps.

Have your fit model try on the garments so you can see if any alterations are needed.

Look over anything you sew with the same critical eye. Noticing mistakes will help you prevent them in the future.

Grading

If you decide, after seeing the sample, that a look works and deserves a place in your line, you may have to get additional patterns made that adjust the garment to fit on different sized bodies. Accessories and some clothing may be "one size fits most."

Grading, or sizing, the pattern up and down is a precision process. Unless you are trained and experienced, hire a professional. Your patternmaker or sewing contractor might be able to recommend a competent local grader, or you might find one with good reviews online.

Legal Considerations

The works you create are a kind of property. As a designer, you have certain rights to that property. You also have the responsibility not to infringe on the property rights of other people.

The fashion design industry is filled with legal and ethical dilemmas: Can you use another designer's line for inspiration? How much do you have to change a pattern to call it your own design? What images and patterns can you use in your designs? How can you protect your designs from being copied?

How to Protect Your Creative Property

Imagine that you have invested months researching, sketching, and sewing your prototypes. Within weeks, an unethical manufacturer copies your designs and puts them in retail stores under his or her label. To protect your creative property and your business, you need to understand your legal rights.

Copyright

A copyright refers to the property rights to an original creative work. The owner of a copyright can publish, reproduce, and sell the work. A piece is automatically protected by a copyright from the moment it is created until 70 years after the creator's death.

Garment styles are not protected by copyright laws. Original textile prints and graphics you create for your designs are protected, and so are original jewelry designs. You can register copyrights through the United States Copyright Office:

U.S. Copyright Office
www.copyright.gov
202-707-3000
101 Independence Avenue SE
Washington, D.C. 20559-6000

Patents

If you develop a new and innovative process for creating your fashions, you can apply for a patent. General garment designs cannot be patented, but some specialty garments with unique ornamentation can. Athletic apparel retailer Lululemon has design patents on some sports bras.

Trademarks

A trademark is a word, name, symbol, or device used to distinguish a product from similar items. A product or process itself is not trademarked. The name, logo, or slogan that identifies the product is the trademark. An example is Ralph Lauren's famous Polo shirt. The embroidered polo player on the chest is trademarked; the shirt design is not.

Trade dress

"Trade dress" refers to the overall look of a product or its packaging that distinguishes and identifies the product, such as the distinctive blue box used by Tiffany & Co. Although trade dress infringement may be more difficult to prove than trademark infringement, designers have successfully used this concept to stop other people from making copies of their creations.

You can apply for patents and register trademarks through the United States Patent and Trademark Office:

United States Patent and Trademark Office
www.uspto.gov
1-800-786-9199
P.O. Box 1450
Alexandria, VA 22313-1450

Copying Designs

Recreating all or part of another designer's work not only exposes you to possible legal action, but it may ruin your reputation in the fashion industry. If your garments are too similar to other designers' looks, you lose the ability to position yourself as innovative or unique.

Using and Altering Patterns

Using a simple commercial pattern as a template for your design is usually acceptable. After all, there are only so many ways to cut an A-line skirt or T-shirt. The finished garment should not look as if it came from the pattern and should require a new pattern to reproduce. Here are some ways to alter a pattern to make it your own:

- Raise or lower the hem

- Add, remove, or move pockets

- Change sleeve shape or length

- Increase or decrease volume

- Add vents, pleats, or darts

- Include structural elements

- Reshape the neckline

- Change the shoulder attachment

- Add trim or details

If you aren't sure whether you should use an existing pattern, check with an attorney who specializes in intellectual property.

Licensed Images and Phrases

If your designs feature an image, name, logo, or pattern associated with another label, an entertainer, a fictional character, a celebrity name, a company, a team, an event, or another past or present entity, you may need to buy the legal rights to use the intellectual material (think Snoopy, Lady Gaga, or the Dallas Cowboys).

When you enter a licensing agreement, you are given certain rights in exchange for payment, usually royalties (percentage of sales price), on the garments you sell.

If you use licensed material, expect to give up some design freedom. You may be required to use certain colors, to reproduce the licensed image only at specific sizes, and to market your garments through certain types of retailers. For example, a celebrity may not want her picture on shirts sold through discount chains.

Did You Know?

In 2015, British retailer Topshop had to pay pop star Rihanna more than $1.8 million for using her picture on a t-shirt without her permission.[6]

Before you use any image, name, phrase, or pattern you didn't make up yourself, have a signed contract with the legal copyright holders. Your licensing agreement should address:

- Time limits: How long will you be licensed to use the intellectual property?

- Cost: How much will you be required to pay in royalties? When will payments be due? Is there a guaranteed minimum you will have to pay regardless of the number of items you sell?

- Marketing limits: How will you be able to market your products?

- Distribution: Where will you be allowed to sell your products? Will there be a minimum price per garment? Are online sales allowed?

- Design limits: What kind of material will you need to manufacture your garments? What design features will be required or forbidden?

6. MailOnline, 2015

- Quality: Will you have to submit to quality testing from the licensor? If so, how often and by whom will the tests be performed?

Because licensing agreements can be so restrictive, you may be tempted to skip the process and use a copyrighted element or change it slightly. This is a bad idea. If you infringe on a protected element from a big company, they will almost certainly sue you, and since they have more money and more lawyers than you, you will almost certainly lose. If you copy other designers, you are sabotaging other people who make their living just like you. Don't put your reputation at stake.

Chapter Six

Selling Your Designs

You have your designs finalized and your samples perfected. Now you need to get your beautiful creations into the hands and onto the bodies of trendsetters.

You have two main options for selling your apparel:

1. Retail — selling directly to consumers

2. Wholesale — selling large quantities at a lower price to retailers like stores who will sell the individual items to the customer

Retail Options

Trunk shows

Trunk shows can be one of the easiest and least expensive ways to reach retail customers. At a trunk show, you can display your entire line to a group of interested shoppers. People can order the styles they like.

Why is a trunk show good for you?

You don't need a lot of inventory.

You can have just one sample of each piece ready for the event, instead of having a variety of sizes in advance. Just be sure to have production quotes before the event so you know how to price the items.

You can fill the room with people who know you and love you.

Get your confidence up, and get people who already support you invested in your products. Invite people you know, and invite them to bring a friend to grow your network of likely customers.

Why is a trunk show good for customers?

It feels exclusive.

Think of how you would feel if you got an invitation to an event with a very small number of tickets – special, right? People like to feel they are in on something special that others don't have access to.

Why is a trunk show good for you and the customers?

It gives you a chance to interact.

Some customers are willing to invest in a quality, high-priced item, or a one-of-a-kind piece, if they know the designer. A trunk show is your opportunity to explain your designs to a ready and willing clientele. Remember, you don't want a one-time sale. You want them to become loyal customers who identify with your brand.

Use a trunk show to get feedback from nice people who want you to succeed. Be ready to make some notes on what they like and don't like about your designs. They could have valuable ideas to help you make modifications.

Did You Know?

Stella & Dot, an *Inc.* magazine 500 fastest-growing company, sells their line of women's accessories mostly through in-home trunk shows. CEO Jessica Herrin started the company at age 24.[7]

Where should you have a trunk show?

Several types of venues are suitable for a trunk show. You could hold one in a retail space, like a clothing store or accessories boutique. If you plan on wholesaling to a particular store, an after-hours trunk show can help you and the owners see how customers respond to your designs.

You could hold a trunk show in someone's home. Do you have a close friend or family member who would be willing to host the event? It's customary to extend a percentage of the evening's sales or credit toward future purchases to the hosts of private showings.

If you decide to hold a trunk show, but don't have an offer for a rent-free space, you could rent a common area, such as a meeting room at an apartment complex clubhouse, community center, or library. There may be space available in a local shopping mall. If you go this route, look for a location that will attract customers in your target market and choose a time when there will be foot traffic.

7. Stella & Dot, 2016

For a trunk show, like any other event, always get the details in writing. Even when doing business with someone you know, having a written contract signed by both parties protects your interests, and makes sure everyone understands what is expected. The contract with the host should address exactly where and at what time the trunk show will begin and end, the percentage of sales the host is entitled to, and any fees involved. In addition, make sure both parties understand their responsibilities, including:

- Who will provide models?

- Who will set up and clean up the venue?

- What kind of marketing will you each provide?

- What kind of refreshments will be provided? Who will be responsible for arranging and paying for the refreshments?

- Will additional lighting be needed? If so, who will provide it?

Before the trunk show, make sure all your samples are clean, repaired, pressed, and stored to prevent wrinkles and damage. If you will be using models, get their sizes so your samples can be altered if needed. If you will not be using models, make sure that there will be appropriate mannequins or dress forms to display your apparel. Prepare marketing materials that promote your line and your business. Have plenty of order forms, business cards, and pens on hand.

Prepare a note card for each piece in your collection. On it, list the construction features, materials used, price, and sizes available. If other colors or variations are available for order, list those as well and prepare swatch books for the customers to review. Be prepared to talk about the inspiration behind each piece and what sets it apart from similar styles.

Give customers an honest estimate of how long they will have to wait for their orders. Make sure the clothes you show will arrive in plenty of time for the appropriate wearing season.

Use the following checklist to help organize your trunk show.

Trunk Show Checklist

- ☐ Negotiate and sign contract with host.

- ☐ Organize event marketing, like social media posts, emails, and flyers.

- ☐ Measure models and fit samples.

- ☐ Repair, alter and press samples.

- ☐ Plan event decorations, refreshments, and seating for guests.

- ☐ Prepare sample note cards.

- ☐ Prepare order forms.

- ☐ Gather marketing supplies, including look books, brochures, catalogs, and business cards.

Online trunk show

What's even easier than a traditional trunk show? A virtual trunk show.

If you're tech-savvy, or know someone who is, you can hold a trunk show online. Just like a traditional trunk show, the online show should be advertised, and should open and close on specific days. Even though posting pictures of your samples on a website won't have the private, "exclusive" feel of a traditional trunk show, potential customers should still feel like they have access to something special that is only available for a limited time.

You can certainly continue to use these photos for your website, but take care to have a unique layout for this one web page to be used only for the trunk show.

Did You Know?

Italian design house Salvatore Ferragamo, known for their luxury shoe line, held their first online trunk show for three weeks in August 2011, offering a limited number of pre-orders for their fall/winter line.[8]

Designer-owned boutiques

If you find that you have a great local following, you are interested in operating a store, and you have the money to open one, you may decide to sell your apparel through your own boutique.

8. Salvatore Ferragamo, 2011

There are several ways you can incorporate a retail store and fashion design. Your store may be the only source of your clothing, or you may also supply to other retailers. You can have a store that only sells apparel from your label, or you may sell other fashions, accessories, and gifts that coordinate with your clothes or appeal to your target market.

If you don't want to jump into a year-long lease for a permanent retail store, you might consider trying a seasonal or transient storefront, sometimes called a "pop-up shop."

- Seasonal stores require a shorter-term lease, as they are only open during specific sale periods. Examples are a kiosk in the mall for a few months before the winter holidays, or a boardwalk kiosk during the summer tourist season.

- Transient stores are an even shorter-term commitment. These are temporary structures that can be set up at fairs, trade shows, or other short term events – like a tent at an arts and crafts show, or a display at an indoor holiday gift sale.

Did You Know?

The pop-up shop, a term first used around the year 2000, is a retail space that opens without advertising, stays open for a few days or weeks, then closes without warning. Even internationally-famous luxury brand Gucci has used pop-up stores.[9]

9. Selfridge & Co., 2016

No matter which type of storefront you choose, the location of your retail shop is a major factor in your profits. A good store location is one that is convenient and popular with your target market. Look for a space that is large enough to show off your designs, but not too large to fill with your inventory.

Before committing to a retail space lease, consider the following questions:

- How much inventory will you have to sell to pay the rent?

- Will you be required to keep your store staffed and open during certain days and hours?

- Will you need to hire additional staff to help operate the store?

- Do you have the time to operate a retail business in addition to your fashion design business?

- Do the businesses around the location support the image you are trying to create for your label?

- Do you have the funds to decorate the space so it appeals to your target market?

- Do you have enough pieces on hand to make the store profitable?

When scouting potential retail space, take notes about the size and shape of each location. List any furnishings or decorations you would need to purchase to make the space reflect the image of your line. Investigate both the foot traffic and the vehicle traffic that pass the location. Pay attention to how easy it is to find the location and whether there is ample room for parking. Visit at least three sites for comparison.

Online sales

If you decide to retail your own clothing, an easy way to start is to sell online. The internet allows new fashion designers like you to show their lines to customers half a world away. If you decide to retail online, you can sell your garments through three basic strategies:

- On your own website and social media

- At online auction sites, like Etsy or eBay

- Through other websites as an affiliate

You can use any or all of these strategies in a combination that works for you.

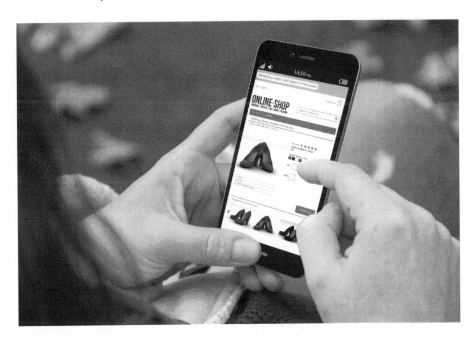

Selling on your own website and social media

Selling on your own website allows you complete freedom in pricing and displaying your clothes. You can design the entire site around the image you want to create for your label.

With so many website builders and templates available, it is easier than ever for you to design your own site, or find a friend to help.

Your social media will be the best marketing for your website. Use your Instagram, Pinterest, and Snapchat photos to display your designs, use hashtags for more exposure, and link your social media accounts to your website.

Use search engine optimization (SEO) to ensure your site shows up in a Google search for your type of products. Luckily, most of the popular website builders like Squarespace and Wix offer wizards to guide you through this process, even if you have a free website account. If you're not familiar with these techniques, you probably know someone who is. Don't be afraid to ask for help. Remember you have a valuable product to trade for services. Do you have a tech-savvy friend who would help with your website in exchange for one of your creations?

Selling on online auction sites

Listing your apparel on internet auction sites, like eBay or Etsy, can help you sell merchandise, bring visitors to your website, and increase customer recognition of your brand. You don't need to carry a large inventory to sell at these sites because you can list each piece individually. Most auction sites have templates you can use to set up your listings.

Many people come to online auction websites looking for bargains, so you may not be able to charge full retail price for your apparel. You have to pay a listing fee, and if you do make a sale, you may have to pay part of the final value on top of that. Even if you don't want to offer your whole line this way, online auctions can be a good way to clear out old merchandise or pieces with sizing or construction flaws. If you are selling seconded inventory, be sure to describe the piece thoroughly so you don't compromise your brand's reputation.

Selling on other sites as an affiliate

As a new designer, you may not get enough traffic to your own website. You might increase your sales by selling as an affiliate on a more established and popular site. Think about the fashion blogs you follow. Is there a blogger who seems like a good fit with your line? Ask if they will link your site. It may take a free sample to get them interested in your product, but if they like your designs it may be worth it. Find out in advance if the host site will take a percentage of the sales price.

Did You Know?

Fashion blogger Julia Engel regularly gets 20,000+ likes for her Instagram ensembles. On her website, **www.girlmeetsglam.com**, she includes links to the stores and designers whose fashions she features.

Have you seen Pinterest pins that say "{affiliate links}"? That means the pin includes links to buy the items shown in the picture, directly from the store or designer who sells them.

Wholesale Options

Instead of selling directly to customers, you may decide to market your designs to retailers, who then sell them to consumers. This is called wholesaling. By selling your line this way, you give up some independence. For example, you will probably not get to choose how the garments are displayed in the store or how they are marketed, but wholesaling saves you the time and money it takes to establish a retail operation.

To wholesale your designs to retail chains, you will need to rent showroom space at a trade show or market center and arrange for corporate buyers to review your line. Competition for large retail contracts is fierce, and buyers from department stores or chain apparel stores may be less likely to take a chance on unknown designers.

If you are thinking about wholesaling, you can learn a lot about the wholesale process by attending trade shows and market weeks.

Did You Know?

Jim's Formal Wear Company, based in Trenton, Illinois, is known as "the largest wholesale formalwear rental company in the world."

Local boutiques are a good place for small fashion designers to start wholesaling. Independent stores are not part of a chain because they want to be different. They offer unique or exclusive products, and may be eager to work with a new designer. Even if the owners are not convinced your line would appeal to their customers, they might be willing to give you some insight about your target market. They may offer to host a trunk show to gauge customer response, or to take some pieces on consignment.

Consignment

When retailers take garments on consignment, they display the clothing for a set period of time or until the clothing is sold. You still own the clothing, and you only receive payment when a customer purchases a garment.

Once the consigned property is sold, the retailer and the designer each get a percentage of the sale price. Usually the designer receives 60 percent to 70 percent of the price and the retailer keeps the rest.

If you can wait for payment, consigning is a way to get more exposure and test the market for your particular styles. For the retailer, it's a low-risk way to add inventory to their shop.

Many designers avoid consignment arrangements because of the financial risk. In a wholesale agreement, the designer gets paid regardless of whether the retailer can sell the apparel or not. Under the typical consignment agreement, the designer only gets paid when the clothing sells.

Pricing Your Product

Whether you sell directly to the consumer or to retail businesses, you should price your pieces before potential customers see them. That makes you look prepared and professional, and you don't risk undercharging for your work.

When pricing your clothes, consider the cost of materials, the amount of time involved in designing, the price of making the patterns and samples, and the manufacturing expenses for each individual piece.

A common retail pricing strategy is to multiply the material and manufacturing costs of each style by 2.2 to 2.8.

For example, if it costs you $15 to purchase the materials and construct your garment, you might set the price between $33 and $42. (15 × 2.2 = 33, 15 × 2.8 = 42).

Only you know exactly how much money you need to cover your expenses including rent, utilities, and equipment. This is just a common formula that helps many designers clear a profit.

Before you set prices for the apparel in your line, do your research. How much are others charging for similar items? If your prices are going to be much higher or lower, be prepared to explain why. If your shirts are more expensive than a similar shirt at a local department store, it may be because you are using a higher-quality, more expensive fabric. Don't be afraid to charge more for higher quality, but be prepared to justify the price.

Chapter Seven

Manufacturing

If you are making single designs, you are a skilled sewer, and you have the right equipment, you can manufacture your clothing yourself. When you begin to get larger orders, you may need to contract out the manufacturing so you can devote more time to designing subsequent lines.

Suppliers

Whether you construct your own garments or use a factory, you need to purchase all the material, fasteners, and trim used in your designs. You can find potential suppliers by visiting trade shows, textile mills, and fabric warehouses. You can also research online fabric wholesalers. Ask the contractor or factory that sewed your samples for recommendations. Talk to other designers about where they like to buy fabric.

If possible, visit several potential suppliers. Make notes and compare purchase minimums, payment terms, return policy, and delivery times. You also may want to ask where the material comes from.

> **"**Manufacturing is an elaborate process, and visiting different factories to observe the production process can be very instructional.**"**
>
> —**Sandhya Garg**, fashion designer
> and *Project Runway* participant

Ask for a sample of all the materials you use, or order a little extra, so you can test the care instructions and make sure they are appropriate.

If you purchase materials in person, be sure to look for color and weave flaws. You can bring your own tape measure to make sure the labeled fabric width is correct.

If you have your purchase delivered, be sure to check the order thoroughly before you use any materials. Check all measurements. Look for flaws in the fabric. Compare what you ordered with what you received.

Manufacturers

Choose your manufacturer with the same care you took to design your line. Ask for recommendations from your suppliers and other designers. Get several quotes before signing a contract.

Keep in mind that the cheapest manufacturing option is not always the best deal. Ask them to give you a list of other clients and check them out. See if you can find out what kind of reputation the factory has, and whether they have experience making clothes like yours. Ask for samples of garments the factory has produced so you can examine their quality.

> **❝**Don't necessarily look for only vendors who can give you 'cheap' product; quality is just as important. One good technique (if you have the bandwidth) to help you secure the best manufacturing partner is to split an order for one item over 2-3 vendors and see who delivers the best in regards to price and quality. Remember, your product is ultimately what will represent your brand.**❞**
>
> — **Monil Kothari**, Founder of Antandre,
> a jewelry e-commerce company

Some manufacturers may have minimum production runs. If you want to place a smaller order, ask if they will lower the minimum number if you are willing to wait longer for your order.

Discuss penalties for late deliveries and coverage of damaged goods. Make sure you are satisfied with the way the manufacturing services contract addresses these issues.

What if you are not satisfied?

If you are not satisfied with a shipment from a supplier or manufacturer, contact the company's sales representative immediately. Stay calm and professional and try to negotiate a replacement or refund. You don't want to alienate suppliers or earn a reputation for being a difficult customer.

Packaging Your Pieces

You've got your finished garments. Now you need to get them to your clients, whether selling directly to consumers or to retailers.

If you are selling to a retail store, they probably have established packing and shipping protocols. Make sure to read their directions carefully. If you ignore their procedures, you risk damaging your working relationship and having your shipments refused.

If you are shipping your clothing directly to your customers, you have more freedom in how you package your garments. Keep in mind that your packing choices reflect your image, and should appeal to your target market.Have you noticed how your monthly *ipsy* subscription delivery comes in the same hot pink bubble envelope? The way you package your products can be an opportunity for you to reinforce your brand.

If you sell high-priced fashions, your customers may expect glossy boxes holding tissue-wrapped products that have been pressed and are ready to wear. If you sell clothes made from organic fibers to environmentally-conscious customers, recycled packing materials may be more appropriate.

Did You Know?

Every purchase from Tiffany & Co., whether in-store or online, comes in their signature Tiffany Blue Box, tied with a white satin ribbon. The term "Tiffany Blue Box" and the color are trademarked.[10]

10. Tiffany & Co., 2016

Although it's not always possible to pack garments so they are ready to wear, take the time to make sure your clothes arrive in the best possible shape. Folding with tissue paper can help soften creases and reduce wrinkling. You can use cardboard to shape garments and keep them looking crisp. Make your customer's first impression a good one.

Include a packing slip in the package so the customer can compare what they received to their order. This is also a chance for you to enclose a catalog or marketing materials so they can see the other products you have to offer.

Labeling

The Federal Trade Commission sets the standards for labeling apparel and household fashions. Most of the requirements are spelled out in the Textile and Wool Acts and the Care Labeling Rule. The purpose of these regulations is to make sure customers know what they are purchasing.

The Textile and Wool Acts

Most textiles and wool products must be labeled with three key pieces of information:

- Fiber content

- Country or countries of origin

- Product manufacturer

These labels must be applied before the finished product is sold to the customer. The labels must be easy to find and read, and must be attached securely. You are required to keep records on the labels you placed on your garments for at least three years.

Fiber Content

If a product is covered by the Textile or Wool Acts, the label must show the generic name of each fiber used, and its percentage of the total fabric. Take a look at the labels on your clothes. You'll see the fibers listed in order of percentage. For example, the label on your favorite jeans might read "80% cotton, 16% polyester, 4% spandex. All the rules are explained in detail on the Federal Trade Commission website, www.ftc.gov.

Country of Origin

All garments and textiles must be labeled to disclose where they were processed or manufactured. You can only use the phrase, "Made in the U.S.A." if every step of your manufacturing process occurs in the United States, and you only use materials that are also from the United States.

If you use products from another country, your label must state where each component came from. A label on a dress, for instance, might read, "Assembled in Mexico. Hemmed in the U.S.A."

Manufacturer Identification

The third type of required information for most garment and textile labels is the name or Registered Identification Number (RN) of the manufacturer. If you don't want to use your company name, you can apply for an RN through the Federal Trade Commission at www.ftc.gov.

The Care Labeling Rule

The Federal Trade Commission also sets rules about listing care instructions on labels.

Textile wearing apparel or piece goods that are used to make wearing apparel are required to have permanent labels with clear care instructions. Some accessories like shoes, gloves, hats, and belts are exempt.

You are required to figure out the correct care instructions for your garments by testing the materials, making sure that your instructions will not cause part of the item to shrink or bleed.

For more information about labeling, contact the Federal Trade Commission at www.ftc.gov.

Chapter Eight
Marketing

Marketing is the art of convincing customers to choose your designs over competitors. If you plan to sell your line to retailers, you will need to convince the boutique owners or store buyers that your styles will appeal to their shoppers. If you sell directly to the consumer, you need to convince them that your apparel is the best value available.

"Selling anything is a challenge. Why is your product better than someone else's? The little details make all the difference. Knowing what your audience likes is important.**"**

— **Ani Hovhannisyan**, wardrobe stylist/editor

Understanding Your Market

Although designing is the fun part, you need to sell your designs to make money. Understanding your target customers, or market, is one of the first and most important steps toward successfully marketing your line.

Look back at the Niche Brainstorming Worksheet you completed in chapter three, where you identified your target market. Understanding as much as you can about these target customers will help you sell to them most effectively. Think about these questions:

- What makes your potential customers different than the general population?

- What are their lifestyle needs?

- Besides clothing, what other things do they spend money on?

- Where do your customers live?

- Where do members of your target market like to shop?

- What is the average age and income of your customers?

The more you know about your customers, the easier it is to create a profitable image and brand.

Image

Your image is how customers see you. You want your target customers to view your products as a better value than the competition. This does not necessarily mean being the cheapest. If you wholesale your apparel to large department stores, you might want the buyers to see your company as one that always meets deadlines and fixes problems quickly and fairly. Even if your clothes are more expensive than another designer, buyers might see yours as a better value because of your reliability.

❝You will be compared to others — fashion designers who have more experience and a different background. Create a persona people can relate to.❞

— **Lindsey Crown**, 4-year Top 10 agency-signed model

Whether an image is good or bad depends on the viewer. For example, consider a designer who sells trendy party clothes. Although the clothes are not made of high-quality material, the styles are a good value to teenagers who want to have the edgiest looks. To their parents, clothes that won't hold up or will be out of style within a few months are wastes of money. If the designer is marketing to teenagers, the image is good.

In the fashion industry, your image is influenced not just by the style and quality of your designs, but by which stores carry your line, your advertisements and reviews, the type of people who wear your products, the customer service you provide, and the cost of your merchandise.

Branding

Companies often use images and words to help consumers differentiate between their products and the competitors. This is called branding. In fashion design, the goal of branding is to have customers recognize and prefer your designs.

Did You Know?

Nike, ranked the 2015 most valuable apparel brand, is based in Beaverton, Oregon.[11]

Branding your apparel is easier if your designs are easy to identify. Think about the Ralph Lauren Polo collection for men. Every shirt, no matter the color or style, has the same embroidered polo player on the chest. If you use a consistent design element on all your pieces, customers will learn to associate that detail with your label.

Branding works hand in hand with image. The best situation is if customers recognize your designs through effective branding and prefer them because of the appealing image.

To develop a brand, first list the attributes of your designs. Attributes are simply the facts about your apparel's construction and style. For example, all your clothing may be manufactured of natural, domestically grown, organic cotton. Next, consider your target market's values. Use these values to turn the attributes into benefits. If your target market is casual, eco-conscious college students, they may appreciate the easy care of organic cotton and the lack of potentially irritating dyes.

After you have identified the benefits to your target market, select a name, logo, or slogan that captures that benefit. If you are stressing the easy care of the fabric, perhaps a slogan like, "less time in the laundry room, more

11. New York Times, 2015

time for fun." An eagle or variation of the flag could remind customers about the domestically grown material. A stylized river or globe sums up the environmental benefits of the line.

Strengthening Your Image and Brand

Place your clothing in stores that also support the benefits your target market wants. If your customers want the most contemporary European-inspired styles, they may skip a designer whose clothing is carried at a big-box superstore.

To build a strong brand, make sure your future designs incorporate the same benefits customers associate with your label. For example, once consumers begin to recognize your signature hardware is on high-quality leather, , if you begin to put the same hardware on cheap synthetics you may devalue the brand.

"Branding is key; it's one of your best tools to stand out. Every day I ask myself, 'Why would a customer buy from me rather than Amazon?' The day I can't answer that question is the day I have to reevaluate my business model.**"**

— Monil Kothari, Founder of Antandre,
a jewelry e-commerce company

Choosing a Name

Another important decision you have to make early in your planning is the name for your fashion design business. What you call your business may influence many other future decisions, such as your logo, marketing image, and website address.

Start by making a list of possibilities. You can include some variations of your own name, lists of your favorite colors, animals, places, and even foods. Use this list to develop different combinations. You will be seeing your business name daily. It will appear on your tags, receipts, and packages, so cross off any choices you do not like.

Did You Know?

Designer Kate Spade left her namesake company in 2007, after selling it to Neiman Marcus. She co-founded a new accessories brand, Frances Valentine, which launched in 2016.[12]

Now search the internet or use a trademark search service to find out which choices are already being used by other companies. The United States Patent and Trademark Office has an online database of pending and granted trademarks that you can access at www.uspto.gov. You want your business name to identify you, not to confuse potential customers or send them to a competitor.

Think about your target customers. Would any of the choices left on your list offend them? Cross those names off. Are any particularly appealing or memorable? Consumers tend to remember names that are descriptive, humorous, or unexpected.

Think about the image you want for your business. Do you want potential customers to see you as artsy, earthy, sophisticated, fresh, or sexy? The name you choose should reflect that image.

12. Frances Valentine, 2016

You may want to register your business name as a trademark with the United States Patent and Trademark Office at www.uspto.gov.

Developing Your Logo

A logo can be a powerful branding tool. You can use your logo on apparel hangtags and labels, on the clothing itself in the form of prints, appliqués, or hardware, on your company website, in public relations events, and on marketing and advertising material. A well-designed logo reinforces your image and helps customers recognize your company.

A study published in 2015 showed the top three most memorable logos in the U.S. were Nike, Apple, and McDonalds.[13] That makes sense; everyone recognizes the swoosh, the apple, and the golden arches. The Amazon "a", the Target bullseye, and the Starbucks mermaid also made the top 10.

Since your logo will stick with you for a long time, take some time to get the design right.

Be sure your design looks good in both color and black and white so you can use it in a variety of graphical settings. If

you have a friend skilled in graphic design, or you can afford to hire a graphic artist, they will know how different fonts and graphics can be combined to create a certain image, and help you develop ad layouts that will work well with your logo.

13. Siegel + Gale, 2015

Online Marketing

A professional website and coordinated social media presence are valuable marketing assets for a new fashion design company. Through your website, you can communicate with potential customers and show off your latest styles. Even if you are on a tight budget and working out of your bedroom, your website can give your business an image of glamour and sophistication. You can have an unlimited number of gorgeous pictures of your designs on your Instagram and Pinterest accounts. Make sure your website is listed in all your profiles.

Social networks, including Facebook and Twitter, allow you to connect with other people based on common interests, acquaintances, experiences, or geographic location. This networking can be a free and efficient way of creating buzz and interest about your line.

"Social media is huge. It's how you break down the barrier between brand and human. It is the modern-day foundation of a customer-client relationship.**"**

— **Lindsey Crown**, 4-year Top 10 agency-signed model

Email is another inexpensive way to reach a large number of potential customers. Free email campaign tools like MailChimp let you create email lists and design beautiful messages to reach a whole list of potential customers at once. Be sure to only send marketing emails to people who have opted into your mailing list—you don't want to be known as a spammer.

Print marketing

In addition to your online presence, sometimes you want customers to have a printed piece that they can keep to remember your designs.

Look books

If you plan to sell your fashions wholesale, a "look book" is an important direct marketing tool that you can send to boutique owners and buyers for chain stores. You should produce a look book each season to showcase your current collection. Include at least one good picture of each garment in your line.

Your look book needs to support the image of your company. If your image is earthy and laid-back, photographs with urban or formal settings may not work as well as a more natural background. Your look book is a chance to show your line creatively, so there are no hard rules about layouts or binding. It is a good idea to include a description of each piece, as well as your contact information, to make it easy for a customer to make a purchase.

You can produce a look book inexpensively by taking pictures of your clothes on volunteer models, printing full size photos, and sliding them into an attractive folder with a mounted business card.

The photographs you use in your look book should show the movement, detail, and drape of each design. This may require a photographer with experience shooting fashion.

"Look at similar photos of designs, and see what others are doing. Now do something different."

— **Ani Hovhannisyan**, wardrobe stylist/editor

There are some ways to display garments without using a model, but the right body wearing your clothes can show off the line and movement of your design and help support your company's image. For your look book, you can use the same model for every outfit to help cut costs and create unity throughout the publication.

Think about your target market when selecting a model. Choose someone whose look embodies the ideals your customers want for themselves. If you design evening wear, select someone sleek and classy. If you design athletic clothing, use a model who looks fit and strong.

Other print marketing materials

You may also want other printed marketing pieces for specific uses.

Brochures and postcards

These are an easy way to feature photos of your designs, and can be used for any event.

Catalogs

The more often someone sees your designs, the more likely they are to buy.

Press kits/sales kits

These are folders you put together to send to editors and buyers. This is a way to package together your best photos, look books, and any other printed materials about your collection, along with your biography and contact information.

Low-cost marketing ideas

You are your best sales tool. In sales, a common motto is "ABC – Always Be Closing" (as in, closing the sale.) As a fashion designer, you want to always be marketing. That means wearing your designs and mentioning the name of your line when you get compliments. You should always have business cards with you, and brochures or catalogs if you have them.

Everywhere you go is a potential opportunity for marketing. Let everyone know your designs are for sale. Ask the managers of coffee shops, books stores, beauty salons, day spas, and other places where your target customers hang out if you can leave marketing materials on the counter or on a bulletin board.

Try to get your designs worn wherever the public will see them, on the kind of trendy customers you're trying to attract. If you have a good-looking friend who is in a band, gets an award, or is well-known around town, ask to style them in your designs.

Chapter Nine

Publicity

Special events

Special events can be effective ways for you to reach new customers and get media coverage. A local magazine or blogger might review a fashion show. The lifestyle page of the newspaper may list upcoming classes and workshops that interest readers.

There are many ways fashion design businesses can reach out to their communities.

Fashion shows

You don't have to design couture garments or live in a major city to have a fashion show. A fashion show can be held as part of a trade show, in conjunction with a trunk show, or as a charity fundraising event. They give buyers or consumers a chance to see your line, and give you the opportunity to see the response to your new designs.

Staging a fashion show can be expensive, but depending on your budget, image, and target audience, there are many ways to cut costs.

Sponsors

To save money on a location, consider teaming up with another business or with a non-profit organization. Even businesses that are not involved in the fashion industry may be able to provide a free venue in exchange for publicity.

Models

One of the draws of a fashion show is seeing clothing on people. Buyers get to see how the line and fabric of a design work together.

For your fashion show, you can use volunteer models. If your show is part of a charity event, the non-profit organization may want to use donors or staff members as models. If you need additional volunteers, check with local performing art schools and agencies for models who may be willing to work in exchange for modeling credits. Ask friends who enjoy modeling to participate.

Before you recruit models, decide on the look you want. Do you want your models to look sexy, athletic, or innocent? Is your image more urban chic or country casual?

> **"**Take what inspires you, and let it set your soul on fire. Don't hold back in sharing your passion with the world.**"**
>
> — **Lindsey Crown**, 4-year Top 10 agency-signed model

Make sure every model fits your label's image and fits in your clothes. Some minor alterations may be needed, but you probably don't want to make major fitting changes to your samples.

Consider completing model agreements even if you are using volunteers. Having everything in writing may reduce confusion and encourage participants to treat the fashion show seriously.

Promotional strategy

Write out how you will bring people to your fashion show. If you are using a location with a lot of foot traffic, like a popular mall or park, you may draw a crowd with just a few posters. A more secluded venue may require additional publicity, including social media posts, email campaigns, direct mailers, press releases, and flyers at local stores.

Preparing for your show

Do you want your audience to see themselves wearing your designs at the beach or at the club? Do you want to show off the fun color palette of your garments or the sophisticated lines? The music, decorations, and props help create the atmosphere of your show.

The announcer can also help set the tone of the event. Besides having a good speaking voice, the announcer should have some fashion knowledge. Although you should write up a script that describes each outfit and rehearse the show with the models, there may be some delays that require the announcer to improvise. You don't want someone who will get nervous or mispronounce common fashion terms.

Think about the order in which you will show your outfits. Each outfit should be connected to the previous one by a design element or inspiration. Even if the link is too subtle for the audience to identify, it will make your show more cohesive.

Rehearse the models' timing and walking with the music. This helps everyone feel comfortable with their role and minimizes confusion at the show. You can get ideas for hair styles and makeup, and make notes of any additional materials you need.

On the day of the show, schedule plenty of time for last-minute clothing alterations. Check that the sound equipment and lights are positioned correctly. One unplugged cord can cause confusion and delay the show.

The hour before the fashion show starts can be a hectic time. Ask a friend to act as a gofer and help you track down missing accessories, calm nervous models, and run messages to the announcer.

After the show

Double check your samples as they are returned. Make sure you get back all the pieces and accessories.

Leave the venue clean and organized, and put back any furniture you rearranged.

Follow up with any buyers or reporters you invited to the show. Ask if they have any questions about your line or need additional information. Send thank you notes to your announcer, models, and helpers.

The following checklist might help you think through every detail to help your fashion show run smoothly.

Fashion Show Checklist
Location
Book location
Schedule show(s)
Lay out catwalk, audience section, and dressing rooms
Personnel
Announcer
Models
Seamstress
Audio technicians
Lighting technicians
Hair stylists
Makeup artists
Photographer
Cleanup crew
Equipment
Sound system
Lighting
Seating for audience
Furniture in dressing rooms
Equipment double-checked morning of show

Props and Accessories
Music
Script for announcer
Accessories for each outfit
Accessories for runway

Apparel
Samples repaired and cleaned
Samples fitted to models
Each outfit labeled with model's name
Each outfit packed with coordinating accessories

Publicity
Press releases
Postcards
Flyers at local stores
Personal calls to buyers
Follow up calls to reporters

Other
Sewing supplies for emergency repairs and alterations
Snacks and drinks for crew
Extra extension cords and batteries
Duct tape
Marketing materials
Extra accessories and two to three extra outfits
Steamer

Classes and workshops

Many people are interested in learning how to look better or create their own clothing. As a fashion designer, you are a local expert in fashion. Classes and workshops can bring in more cash, attract new customers, and increase brand awareness for your label. An innovative class or workshop can be a newsworthy event, which may mean free publicity.

You could try holding a one-day workshop on one of the many topics that may attract an audience in your area. For example:

- Sewing your own fashions

- Dressing for your body type

- Combining colors and patterns in your wardrobe

- Accessorizing

- Basic alterations

- Building a professional wardrobe

- Designing your dream wedding gown

- Looking your best at the beach

- Going through pregnancy in style

- How to stay ahead of trends

- Modifying the basic T-shirt

Public Relations

The media can be a great way to get free publicity. A glowing review by a fashion blogger can help demand for your styles explode. A newspaper article about your involvement with a local charity helps shape your image.

A press release is a way of announcing news and events to the media. Reporters are looking for good stories, but most do not want to be bombarded with press releases that are not newsworthy.

Before sending a press release, determine which department or reporter would be the best match for the story. Some publications have a directory on their websites or editorial pages. You may want to read several issues of the publication to get a feel for how news is divided among the sections.

Even if you target the right reporter, a press release may be ignored if it does not follow a standard format. The following sample shows correct placement of the title and date, and your contact information. In the body of the press release, include the basic who, what, when, where, and why. Keep it short and to the point.

A good press release may lead to an article, and it can also help you become known in the press as a local fashion expert. If they need information for a future story, they may contact you. Building a relationship with the press can help you get the publicity you need to make your special events successful.

Sample Press Release

FOR IMMEDIATE RELEASE
Contact: Hayley Smith / 999-999-9999 /
hayley@yourdesignbusiness.com

Wedding Fashion Show to Benefit Veterans

Anytown, CA - Local brides will have the chance to see the latest styles of wedding gowns, jewelry, tuxedoes, and flower arrangements during a free event at the White Hills Mall.

Designer Hayley Smith will host the wedding fashion show at 2:00 p.m. on December 1. The show will feature Smith's couture gown collection, as well as jewelry from Silversmith's Diamonds and flowers from Carey Floral Masters.

"Both Silversmith's Diamonds and Carey Floral are known for their cutting-edge designs," Smith says. "We are thrilled to be able to show women the kind of styles that are being seen in Paris and New York this winter."

Smith has been designing custom wedding gowns since 2008.

"Brides want to look beautiful and timeless on their wedding day," she says. "I help make their dream dresses become reality."

Refreshments for the event will be provided by the White Hills Veterans Association, a 501(c) nonprofit organization. Donations for a scholarship fund for children of veterans will be accepted at the event.

"The White Hills Veterans Association has been helping our soldiers and their families since 1958," says Smith. "It is an honor to be able to help them."

For more information or to schedule an interview, please contact Hayley Smith at 999/999-9999 or hayley@yourdesignbusiness.com.

Chapter Ten
Starting a Business

Once you have decided you have the skills and vision needed to make your design business a success, you might feel tempted to break out your sketchbook, go shopping for fabric, and call up some friends to model for your first fashion show.

However, taking some time for a little preparation and planning of your business' future at this stage may save you money, time, and problems later on. As soon as you start selling your designs, the government considers you a business. Now is a good time to think about what kind of business you want to have, and what it will take to get there.

Organizing Your Business

As a business owner, one of the first decisions you need to make is your legal relationship with the business. There are three types of businesses: sole proprietorships, partnerships, and corporations.

Sole proprietorships

If you do not file any paperwork with the government, your business is a sole proprietorship. This means that any profits from the business are your personal income and are subject to income tax. You are responsible for paying all expenses for the business.

Partnerships

You may need the experience, skills, or money of another person or group to get your business started. A partnership offers the convenience of a sole proprietorship with the ability to share the ownership and responsibilities of the business with someone else.

Like sole proprietorships, partnerships are easy to form. Also like sole proprietorships, the parties involved in a partnership are personally responsible for any business debts.

Corporations

Unlike a sole proprietorship or partnership, a corporation is considered separate from its owners for legal purposes, and is owned by stockholders.

Many startup businesses consider another type of corporate structure called a limited liability corporation (LLC). The LLC structure has the limited liability benefits of a corporation, but profit or loss is considered personal income.

Which business type is best for you?

You should consider whether you prefer the freedom to open, operate, and close your business that a sole proprietorship offers or the security of limited personal liability that comes from owning a corporation. A lawyer or tax advisor can help you understand the financial benefits of a particular business structure.

Laws, Regulations, and Licenses

Business regulations differ by state and city. To sell products, you may need to apply for a resale license or sales tax license. You may also need a city or county business license. If you will buy tax-exempt, wholesale supplies, you need to have this number. In addition, you need this number to file sales tax on any goods you sell locally.

If you live in California or New York and are manufacturing the designs you sell, you may need a garment manufacturing license. You can apply for this certificate through your state department of labor.

Research what you will need and how much it will cost. To start a business, you may need to plan for some or all of these licenses and fees:

- Resale license

- Business license

- Garment manufacturing license

- "Doing business as" (DBA) certificate

- Trademark registration

- Incorporation fees

- Insurance

Financing Your Business

Starting your own fashion design business could launch you into your future, but any business takes money and careful planning to get started. Be realistic about how much it will cost, so you can focus on being the creative designer you want to be.

How much money will you need?

Try to make a list of every expense you can think of -- supplies, equipment, licensing, and marketing.

Your design studios may need these basic supplies:

- Sketch books in several sizes

- Drawing pencils, watercolors, colored pencils, or fiber-tip pens

- Loose, high quality drawing paper for final drawings

- Light table for tracing

- File cabinet to organize sketches, clips, and swatches

- Foam boards and adhesives for storyboards

- Rulers, compasses, protractors, and other drafting supplies

- Design or graphics software

- Fabric/fiber

If you will be manufacturing the clothes you sell, you may need the following equipment:

- Sewing machine

- Serger

- Knitting machine

- Linker

- Shelving and storage

- Cutting table

- Workbench

- Directional lighting

- Notions

- Embroidery machine

- Dressmaking or tailor's bust form

- Pattern paper

- Grader's set square

- Fabric/fiber

You may also need some of these general office supplies:

- Computer

- Stationery

- Desk and chair

- Fax machine

- Scanner

- Printer

- Copy machine

- File cabinet

- Planner or wall calendar

- Accounting/tax software

Where can you cut costs?

You might find good deals on used office furniture, manufacturing equipment, and supplies at thrift stores, auctions, and liquidation sales.

If you plan to start small, you may be able to get by with "hobbyist equipment"—machines manufactured and marketed toward the home sewer. Hobbyist equipment may not be as durable or versatile as professional or industrial machines, but it is significantly less expensive and may be suitable until you can afford to upgrade.

You may also be able to rent expensive equipment or share the cost with another designer. If this is not possible, consider contracting out work instead of buying highly specialized machines.

Types of financing

The reason most business dreams never become reality is a lack of money. If you honestly believe in your talent and skills and are committed to making your business a financial success, you can find a way to secure the funds you need.

Personal savings and income

If you work or have savings, using your own money is a great way to start your business, since you have complete control over how the money is used. The downside is that there is no guarantee your fashion design business will make money at first or at all. Although knowing that your hard-earned cash is on the line can keep you motivated, it can also be stressful.

Private loans

Private loans include money from family or friends that is given with the expectation of repayment. A parent, relative, or family friend is the most likely place to look for a loan. Just know the lenders may assume that their investment entitles them to input in your business decisions. If you don't pay them back on time, you may hurt the relationship.

If you decide to accept a private loan, make sure that both you and the lender agree to the terms, including the length of the loan, interest rate, amount and schedule of payments, and rights of the lender. It's almost important to make this kind of agreement in writing. Consider having it notarized as well to add a sense of seriousness to the exchange.

Personal credit cards

Personal credit cards are a fast and easy way to purchase equipment, pay bills, or even access cash. Minimum monthly payments are usually low, but credit cards usually have a higher interest rate than bank or personal loans. If you make a payment late, your interest rate may go up so you owe even more money. A high balance on a credit card can be hard and expensive to pay off, especially if you are only paying the minimum monthly payment.

Business loans

Getting a bank loan is difficult for any first-time business owner. Banks prefer to lend to people with a proven track record of making money and paying back their debts. Without a well-researched business plan, good personal credit history, and appropriate collateral, securing a bank loan isn't likely.

The Small Business Association (SBA) can help business owners secure bank loans by guaranteeing the repayment. Read more information about receiving a guaranteed loan at www.sba.gov.

Nonprofit Organizations

Some nonprofit organizations give business owners grants or low-interest loans if the business meets specific qualifications based on ethnicity, geographic location, gender, or income. Another great benefit is that these organizations provide mentoring programs, workshops, and educational materials to help new business owners succeed.

The SBA has a microloan program for loans of less than $35,000, which includes training and help to the business owner.

The SBA's nonprofit resource partner, SCORE, matches new small business owners with volunteer mentors, who can help you find funding and resources, and they offer free online materials and workshops at www.score.org.

Did You Know?

SCORE has more than 11,000 volunteer business leaders who helped start more than 53,000 new businesses in 2015.[14]

Business plan

A business plan is a formal, written document that explains how a business will run. It covers the financial, operational, and marketing details and future goals of the business. If you need to borrow money or apply for a grant to start your business, you will need to write a business plan.

Creating a business plan can help you organize your ideas, see how they fit together, and determine reasonable goals for the near future and for the

14. SCORE Association, 2016

long term. Once you have a working business plan, it can serve as a map to keep your business on track.

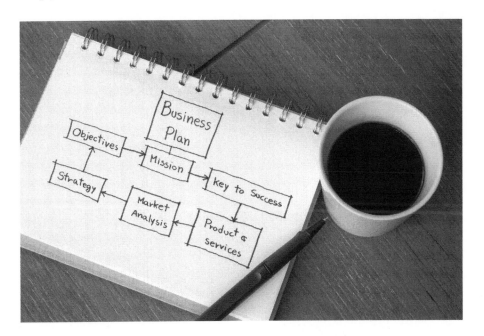

What do you need to write a business plan?

You will need to collect or create the following documents:

- Résumés for all owners, showing work, education, professional affiliations, honors related to fashion, and any special skills.

- Financial statements for all owners, including lists of assets, income, and expenses.

- Personal and business credit reports for all owners.

- Copies of equipment or property leases.

- Letters of reference from business associates or other people who can assess your professional skills. Avoid using family members.

- Copies of current business contracts, such as purchase orders or loans.

- A copy of your business license.

- A copy of your insurance policy.

- The business's articles of incorporation or partnership agreement.

- Trademarks.

- Licensing agreements.

- Any research you have gathered about your target market.

Parts of a Business Plan

A business plan should use the following standard organization:

1. Cover sheet

2. Executive summary

3. Statement of purpose

4. Description of business

5. Industry overview

6. Competition analysis

7. Marketing strategy

8. Operating procedures

9. Personnel

10. Financial data

Good sources for fashion industry information include:

- U.S. Department of Labor, Bureau of Labor Statistics (**www.bls.gov**)

- The American Apparel and Footwear Association (**www.apparelandfootwear.org**)

Good sources for help writing a business plan include SBA (**www.sba.gov**), SCORE (**www.score.org**), and your local library and chamber of commerce.

CASE STUDY: EMILY COSTA
Founder/Designer of Rebel Redefined,
21 years old

@emilycosta
@rebel_redefined
www.rebelredefined.com

Fashion has always been a huge interest of mine, and it's hard to think of a time when it wasn't! When I was younger, I found a real joy in dressing up and experimenting with my own individual style. For me, there was always something very unique and special in the ability to convey who I was as a person through my style.

Growing up, I always had an entrepreneurial spirit that really developed and took over while I was in high school. During those years, I dedicated myself to learning as much as I could about the fashion industry as a whole. I was consistently inspired by the idea of owning my own brand.

Two things really prepared me for this venture; one was attending Teen Vogue's Fashion University in New York City in 2011 for the first time at age 16. The other was taking a pre-college intensive course at the Fashion Institute of Technology in New York City on how to start and manage a small business. I used the knowledge I learned from successful designers like Michael Kors and Alexander Wang that spoke at Teen Vogue's Fashion U and the lessons I learned at FIT that summer and applied them to make my vision come to life.

I was 17 when I launched my brand Rebel Redefined. That same year, my brand was sold on NYLON magazines shop, featured in many articles, and worn by celebrities. I think my brand gained popularity so fast because it came from an authentic vision. People from all over the world really connected with the concept of the brand, which has always been fun, edgy, and a testament to being yourself.

I had to learn every aspect of running a business while preparing to launch. I did a lot of extensive research to figure out what would be the best ways to manage Rebel Redefined and the vision I had. I figured out how to design a website on my own, I contacted local printing shops to figure out how to manufacture our products, and I learned about marketing techniques to get the brand in the public eye. I read tons of books and articles online to make sure I understood what went into a successful business.

An important lesson I've learned is that there is a lot of trial and error — especially when first starting out. You have to see what works best for your vision and what will be the most effective!

Truthfully, I still am learning every single day, but that is one of the joys of owning your own company. Every day is a new adventure, and you are forever growing as a designer and entrepreneur!

There is always going to be some hesitation when starting something new, going out on a limb to join the fashion industry, or creating your own brand. The biggest piece of advice I wish I would have known early on is that no one successful started out there. They have worked tirelessly to get to that success, and they have probably experienced many failures along the way. Those failures are what shape the path to success! Your vision is worth bringing to life, and you can make it happen. It just takes patience, hard work, and vigilance.

Even if you feel you are too young to start your career, it is still worth a try. I was always under the impression I would not be successful at launching my own company until I was much older, but I surprised myself. Age is just a number; experience and knowledge can begin at anytime!

Chapter Eleven
Customer Service

As a fashion designer, your best customer is a repeat customer. Just like any business, you need to earn a reputation for good customer service. Customer service includes any procedure and interaction that affects a customer's purchasing experience.

If you've ever worked at a retail store or restaurant, you've probably had some customer service training, and you know that it's more than "the customer is always right."

Why is customer service important?

The customer service you provide is one of your most important marketing tools. Your customers will share their purchasing experiences, good or bad, with each other. They will review you on Facebook or Yelp, and they will call you out on Instagram and Twitter. A reputation for poor customer service can reduce your sales, and make wholesale and retail buyers less willing to take a chance on you.

The customer service you provide can help your line stand out in the fashion industry. As a small business, you may be able to be more flexible than the larger, more established companies. If a buyer has a problem with a garment or a special request for alterations or packaging, you are able to deal with the customer directly and find a solution. In larger companies, the customer may have to deal with multiple management layers.

Good customer service goes beyond making sure people who purchase your designs are satisfied. Everyone who attends a trunk show, visits your retail space, or attends one of your workshops is a potential customer. Just because they don't buy today doesn't mean they never will.

Addressing customer concerns

Some customer service concerns are specific to the fashion industry. Being aware of these issues can help you establish procedures to try to prevent them. Because of human error, manufacturing issues and material flaws, mistakes will likely happen. Having written plans to deal with common problems can help you provide good customer service.

Sizing

Garment sizing for women's fashions is confusing, since there is no standard size scale.

If you sell to more than one retail store, you may find it hard to match the size standards of each. What is sold as a size 8 in one store may be a size 2 in another. One way to match several different scales is to label your garments with actual measurements, similar to men's clothing.

If you retail your own designs, consider offering to exchange garments or refund the purchase price when customers return clothing because of sizing problems.

Fit

Some garments have disproportionate measurements that cause fit rather than sizing issues. For example, a customer may return a pair of jeans that fits in the waist and inseam but is too wide in the hips. Most fit complaints can be resolved by refunding the purchase price when the garment is returned.

Care labeling

The instructions you provide for washing, drying, and ironing your designs should minimize the chance of damage, fading, color bleeding, and shrinkage. Make sure you test your instructions on the finished garment.

Packaging

Customers may complain if a garment arrives wrinkled, stretched, or damaged because of the packaging. Complaints about poorly packaged items can be handled by offering to replace the damaged goods or refund the purchase price.

Planning and experience can help reduce packaging-related complaints. Try folding lightweight garments around cardstock or cardboard to help the fabric keep its shape. Reinforce collars with shapers. Tape foam around trim that may get crushed during shipping. Wrap folded garments in plastic to protect them.

Label placement

Customers may complain if the care instructions, fiber content, manufacturing identification, and country of origin labels on your garments are hard to find or uncomfortable. Avoid layering tags, which can cause stiff seams, bulges, and pressure points. Tags placed where they are likely to rub the wearer's skin, such as at the back of the neck or waistband, should be soft and flexible.

Workmanship

Depending on the complexity of a style, there may be many places where manufacturing errors can occur. For example, the hem of a skirt might hang awkwardly, a zipper on a pair of pants might not stay up, or there might be missing stitches in a seam. In many cases, garments returned because of workmanship-related concerns may be repaired and returned to the retail floor. Whenever possible, inspect finished garments before they are sold.

Color

Customers may be dissatisfied with a garment if the color is not what they expected. This is primarily a problem for internet or catalog sales where monitors and printer ink may not reproduce colors accurately.

In addition to showing pictures of each garment and color choice in your print or online catalog, consider adding descriptions of the hues, like "royal blue" or "candy apple red."

Material flaws

Color, texture, and printing inconsistencies on fabric or trim may be the result of improper handling or flawed material. You can minimize complaints about material flaws by thoroughly inspecting all fabric, fasteners, decorations, and trimmings that you purchase.

Shipping

Customers may complain about slow or over-priced shipping. To help reduce shipping-related issues, offer customers choices in delivery time and cost, and link to cost estimators provided on delivery companies' websites.

Exchanging garments and refunds

If a customer wants to exchange a garment for another size, style, or color, there may be questions about who pays for returning the unwanted merchandise and sending the replacement.

Having written return and exchange policies can help minimize disputes about shipping payment. If a customer is returning a garment because of a manufacturing error or material flaw, paying the postage both ways can help increase their satisfaction with the transaction.

Developing customer service policies

After you decide how you will solve common customer service issues, take the time to put your policy in writing and make it available to your customers and employees.

A customer service policy should address specific actions that will be taken in response to common situations. The policy should lay out the responsibilities of the customer as well as those of the business.

Some issues to address in the customer service policy include ordering, payment, shipping, returns, and customer privacy. Make sure to include details. Your policy should try to reduce customer confusion and frustration.

Ordering

In your customer service policy, list all the ways customers can order your products. Include contact information for each ordering method. If you accept telephone orders, include your telephone number. If you send out catalogs or sales kits, tell potential customers how to get on your mailing list.

Payment

List the different ways customers can pay for their orders. If different sales terms apply for certain methods, be sure to include the details. List the credit cards you can process in addition to any online payment services you accept, like PayPal. If you will allow wholesale customers to buy on credit, list the qualification and payment terms.

Shipping

In addition to listing the different carriers and delivery options from which your customers can choose, include the approximate time it will take you to fill orders.

Returns

Your written return policy should include how long a customer has to return a garment and the paperwork that should accompany any returns. Describe who is responsible for shipping costs under different circumstances.

In your written policy, include the procedures customers should follow to initiate a return. Give the address where they should send the merchandise and any forms that need to be completed. Provide estimates regarding how long customers will have to wait for their refunds.

Special concerns for custom designers

If you sell custom, one of a kind, or "wearable art" garments, you may have some additional customer service considerations. Since you are constructing something unique (and probably expensive) for that customer, you will have a closer relationship with your clients. Providing outstanding customer service will be very important.

Simply talking through the details with clients can prevent a lot of customer service issues with custom designs. Keep emails, and keep notes of phone conversations.

Some points you may want to clarify with your client include:

- **Is the outfit for a special event?** If so, make sure you will be able to get the finished garment to the customer well before the event's date. Clarify how formal the event will be and the expected weather.

- **How many times does the client intend to wear the garment?** Clothing that will be worn and laundered multiple times may need different construction considerations than a garment that will only be worn once and then packed away.

- **How does the client intend to care for the garment?** If the customer does not like to hand wash or dry clean their clothes, your fabric and construction choices will be limited.

- **Does the client have any special needs?** If the garment will be used for a performance or sporting event, you may need to use technical fabrics and sturdier construction. If the client has a limited range of motion, you may need to size and place fasteners and openings carefully.

- **What image does the client want to project while wearing the garment?** Does he want to look sexy, professional, casual, or mature?

- **What body or facial features does the client love about herself? What does she want to hide?** The cut and design features you choose can draw the viewer's eye to or away from certain areas.

Time Issues

For custom fashion businesses, meeting deadlines is a constant challenge. If you realize that you are not going to meet a deadline, you have several options. You can sacrifice the quality of the garment by taking design or construction shortcuts to make up for lost time. Although this strategy can help you meet the deadline, your customer may still end up disappointed if the final product does not meet her expectations.

Another option is to be up-front with your client about the status of her project. If she is not planning to wear the garment for an upcoming event, she may not mind granting a deadline extension. If time is critical, the client might have some preferences of what can be cut or changed to help finish the garment quickly. For example, you may be able to redesign a formal gown to need less beading or to have a less intricate hem line.

When preparing an estimate for a custom order, consider adding extra time to allow for mistakes and unforeseen events that can put you behind schedule. No one will complain if an order is finished early!

Delivery Issues

Because custom items can be difficult or impossible to replace, take extra care when packing and shipping orders. Make sure that fragile parts of a garment, such as buttons or glass beading, are protected with appropriate wrapping and cushions. Consider purchasing insurance with your shipping service.

Quality issues

Once they see the finished products, customers may not be completely happy with the results. The color might not be what they expected, the fabric might not be as soft or heavy as they hoped, or the craftsmanship may not be as exquisite as they were led to believe.

If a customer complains to you about the quality of their order, take their comments seriously. Talk with your client and try to find the heart of the problem. If the fit is uncomfortable or incorrect, offer to alter the garment. If the color is wrong, determine if you can safely dye the garment. Decorations, fasteners, seams, and hems can sometimes be altered without much trouble.

If your client is disappointed with the craftsmanship of the piece, find out all the details you can about where the construction fell short of expectations. Fix the garment if possible. If not, consider offering a full refund upon the return of the garment.

Remember to stay calm and not to take the criticism personally.

The best way to prevent quality issues is to describe your designs accurately. Avoid exaggerating the material, style, or workmanship. Correct any errors you find before the garment leaves your workshop. Fix even tiny flaws. Be a perfectionist when it comes to your clothes. It is your reputation that is on the line.

The hard-to-please customer

If you have ever worked with customers, you know that occasionally a client won't seem satisfied with anything. Keep the following pointers in mind when dealing with a difficult customer:

- Stay calm. You are more likely to work out a solution if the encounter does not turn into a screaming match.

- Act professional. Resist the urge to vent to other customers.

- Breaking your policies can be the solution, but it can cause new problems. Once a customer gets special treatment, they may expect it every time.

- Try not to take complaints personally. Although it can be hard to separate yourself from something you designed or created, it can be easier to deal with a problem if you don't consider it an insult on your talent or abilities.

- Take a timeout. If you are getting too upset by a situation, take a few minutes to yourself before returning a call or email from a disgruntled customer.

Although most customers are willing to work with designers to fix problems, there are a few who can always find something else to complain about. You will have to decide when it is in the best financial interest of your business to stop trying to please a difficult customer.

Conclusion

Get Your Design On Now!

Now that you have all the information, are you ready to make your dream a reality?

Fashion design school, competitions, and starting your own brand are great long-term goals, but what can you do to start right now?

Social Media

You're already on social media, so use it to launch your brand. Celebrities like Rihanna, Justin Bieber, and Miley Cyrus have brought instant attention to unknown designers they saw on Instagram, so make sure your designs are there to be discovered, and don't be afraid to tag the celebrities you'd like to see wearing your styles.

Start a vlog

You have a smart phone. You can start a YouTube channel.

Short videos can be a great way to showcase your looks. Put your BFF in your favorite design and show it off, or demonstrate a DIY hack like your favorite way to tie a scarf or decorate a hat. The more videos you post, the more comfortable you will be, and the more followers you can attract.

YouTube vlogger Bethany Mota, who started making short videos in her bedroom when she was 13 years old, now, at age 20, has her own line at Aeropostale.[15]

Write a blog

You would rather write than be a video star? No problem – start a blog.

Well-known blog site WordPress and many other hosting sites allow you to create a free website for your blog using their templates. You could start your blog by simply posting on Facebook to announce your new looks and designs.

Post pictures

A picture is worth 1,000 words. Use Instagram and Pinterest to post photos of your designs, and to showcase your style. Use well-known Instagram hashtags like #OOTD and Pinterest tags like "Fashion" to get more exposure.

Learn

School

Your high school might not have a fashion design, or even a graphic design class, but that doesn't mean there's nothing to learn. A basic art class can help you learn valuable sketching techniques and allow you to practice

15. Forbes, 2016

putting colors and designs together. Your art teacher could be valuable in helping you compile your first portfolio.

Online learning

Take advantage of the internet's ability to connect you to experts around the world.

University of Fashion (**www.universityoffashion.com**) offers online lessons on a variety of topics, from sketching to sizing to styling, taught by top fashion school professors, and many are free.

Seventeen magazine posts their "quick and easy fashion DIY videos" on their website (**www.seventeen.com**), with topics like "How to Turn Your Favorite Outfit Into a Super Cute Costume" and "7 Fab New Ways to Wear Denim This Week."

Volunteer

Costuming

Most community theater groups and school drama departments would love to have your help with draping and costuming. This could be a fun way for you to get experience sewing and fitting, and maybe learn something about creating historical or unique costumes. Chances are you'll be working alongside a knowledgeable costume designer who can help you learn the ropes. Either way, this kind of experience will look good on a college application or résumé.

Fashion shows

Volunteer to organize or help with a fashion show as a fundraiser for a school club or your favorite charity. This is a way to help out a worthy cause, and get some real-life fashion show experience.

Hold a costume fashion show before Halloween, or a prom fashion show before students start shopping for the big dance. Let's face it, students need fashion advice, and they need to see you as their fashion expert.

Just Do It.

You're already a fashionista. Now be a fashion designer!

Guest Contributors

Ani Hovhannisyan is the founder of couture bridal styling agency Through The Veil. With a focus on weddings, engagement parties, and bridal showers, Ani has quickly become a thought leader and influencer in the New York City bridal scene. Prior to finding her niche, Ani's styling appeared in editorial spreads across international publications including Elle, Glamour, NYLON, and Vogue, while her bridal work has been featured in Cottage Hill, Lovely Bride, Well Wed, and more.

As a consultant, she has styled public figures for numerous red carpet events, and predicts seasonal accessory, footwear, and fashion trends that are put into motion on both the catwalk and on the New York City streets. Ani works with the industry's top designers, seamstresses, photographers, and wedding planners to provide customers with an unparalleled full-service styling experience. She believes a wedding is the most important fashion event of a bride's life, and though perfection is subjective, "ordinary" simply will not do.

For more information on Ani Hovhannisyan and Through The Veil, visit **www.throughtheveil.nyc**. For press and booking inquiries, please contact Sarah ElSayed, sarah@throughtheveil.nyc.

Deanna Kei is a NYC based Designer, Stylist, and Fashion Illustrator. She loves designing for all sorts of categories and occasions and has worked in Contemporary Sportswear, Outerwear, Juniors, Childrenswear, and Menswear. She's done styling for both individuals and photo shoots and has illustrated for TV commercials, online magazines, market week promos, and fashion bloggers. Just recently, her first book illustrations were published in *The International Fashionista's Lookbook Diary*. Her favorite color is purple.

On the day of her high school graduation in 2013, **Emily Costa** launched Rebel Redefined. It is the ultimate online destination for unique tees and tanks. Each design is made to embody the spirit of being who you are and express yourself through what you wear. The name Rebel Redefined was inspired by the vision of redefining and rebelling against society norms in all aspects and becoming the truest version of yourself. Today, Emily continues to manage the brand and lives in New York City where she is getting a degree in both Fashion Business Management and Marketing at the Fashion Institute of Technology.

Photo Credit: Casey Jade Photography

Las Vegas Fashion designer **Ermelinda Manos** was born in southern Albania and raised in Athens, Greece. She moved to Las Vegas at the young age of twelve and has called Sin City home ever since. Manos received her bachelor's degree in fine arts and fashion design from the International Academy of Design and Technology, as well as an associate's of arts degree in philosophy from the College of Southern Nevada.

Learning and gaining experience from the best, Manos honed her skills in the fashion industry by working with world-renowned brands such as Giorgio Armani Prive, Chanel, Teen Vogue, Macy's Passport, Nordstrom's, and Miss Universe as a dresser. After spending time as a fashion stylist, Manos fulfilled her childhood dream of designing her own label, which focuses on handmade women's evening gowns, cocktail dresses, and bridal attire. She launched her women's eveningwear line, Ermelinda Manos Designs, at LA Fashion Week in the fall of 2009. Following the launch of her line she was named one of the most anticipated designers of Los Angeles Fashion Week.

Julie Hunot began her design career working at Dreamgirl International in 2002, the summer before her senior year at Otis College of Art & Design. After graduating from Otis with honors and appearing on the first-ever student cover feature of Apparel News, Julie was hired on the spot as Dreamgirl's secondary designer. As Dreamgirl continued to grow, the company started hiring more and more designers for both the lingerie and costume divisions, which shifted Julie's role into a more management-focused position, and she was eventually promoted to Vice President of Lingerie Development & Design.

Although Julie never went to school specifically for lingerie and never imagined she would spend her entire career designing for the same company, she is still Dreamgirl-loyal after 13 years. She says of her evolution at the company: "Dreamgirl is, in a lot of ways, still a small company, so the designer role still encompasses many areas that maybe a 'traditional' designer job might not be responsible for, but I wouldn't have it any other way. I love the fact that we have so much freedom as designers, and we really get to be a part of the vision from the very beginning when we put pen to paper (Yes; I still sketch old-school with markers and paper!) through the end result seeing the garment in print for our catalog."

At the age of 16, **Lindsey Crown** moved into a model's apartment on South Beach where she signed with Wilhelmina Models; from there, she moved to Los Angeles where she was signed with Vision L.A. She then moved to New York City where she signed with Major Model Management and finally Mexico City where she signed with Paragon Model Management.

Lindsey worked for various brands such as Steve Madden, Hollister, Bumble and Bumble, Aeropostale, and Nylon Magazine over the four years she spent in the industry. Eventually, she became exhausted of the fashion industry and was ready to work towards something more. She now attends school at the University of Florida as a public relations and creative photography student.

Lisa Dixon, currently the Design Director of Lingerie at Dreamgirl International, has a diverse background in design that began in the mid-1990's at a Miami-based wholesaler, where she was responsible for the design of children's swimwear and the development of a men's woven and knit golf-focused clothing collection. From there, she moved into designing lingerie, sleep, and loungewear for private label collections (IE: collections designed for specific chain and specialty stores.), which led to a position designing and branding the men's lifestyle divisions at Sears, Roebuck and Co. After her time at Sears, she took a position designing swimwear for the re-launch of Cole of California and from there, moved into senior designer positions for two major brands – Lands' End and Jantzen. Her swimwear was featured in a variety of top-tier media outlets, ranging from Vogue to Sports Illustrated to Good Morning America. In 2011, Lisa accepted a position at Dreamgirl International. She is currently one-half of the team that is responsible for setting the overall "tone" and "look" of each Dreamgirl Collection, and is involved in all the aspects of the design process from start to finish.

Maureen (Molly) Demers is a Costume Designer/Shop Manager in Ocala, Florida. When earning her bachelor's degree in theater education, she "fell madly in love" with costuming while taking a costume history class. She received a Master of Fine Arts degree in costume design and technology from the University of Florida and has worked as a draper and costumer for professional theater companies including Denver Center for the Performing Arts. Molly's specialties include costume design, draping, construction, wig maintenance and wardrobe.

Photo Credit: Annabella Charles Photography

A former Shark Tank contestant, **Moziah "Mo" Bridges** is the 14-year-old CEO of Mo's Bows handmade bowties: a Memphis family-run business. Mo's bowties have been featured in numerous international publications, and are sold online at **mosbowsmemphis.com**, as well as Neiman Marcus and other retailers throughout the United States.

Monil Kothari, a third generation diamond jeweler and serial entrepreneur, founded Antandre in 2014. Monil spent two years training throughout India and the U.S. to master his lapidary and design skills. Previously, Monil was the founder of a digital marketing company, building marketing tools for local, small businesses. Monil earned his undergraduate degree from Bentley University and is GIA accredited.

Sandhya Garg is a London College of Fashion alumna and has worked at Alexander McQueen, Gucci, Liberty London, and Alice Temperley, amongst others. She was recently seen on Season 13 of Project Runway, where she impressed judges with her unique point of view and won two challenges. Sandhya has shown her unique collections at Mercedes-Benz New York Fashion Week, and the brand has been featured in Marie Claire US, Ftv. com, Elle Magazine, and Cosmopolitan Magazine, to name a few.

You can find more about Sandhya's design process on her website at **www. sandhyagarg.com** or on Instagram at sandhyagarg11. She is also a Fashion Illustration professor at MassArt, Boston and has a design studio at Joy Street Artists Studios, MA.

Bibliography

"Fashion Designers." U.S. Bureau of Labor Statistics. U.S. Bureau of Labor Statistics, May 2015. Web. 13 Nov. 2016.

"The Trend Forecast." Interview by Avery Trufelman. Audio blog post. 99percentinvisible.org. Radiotopia, 20 Sept. 2016. Web. 15 Nov. 2016.

"Website Policies." Trademarks & Copyrights | Tiffany & Co. Tiffany & Co., 2016. Web. 05 Dec. 2016.

Frances Valentine. "About - Frances Valentine." Frances Valentine About | Introduction. Frances Valentine, 2016. Web. 05 Dec. 2016.

Friedman, Vanessa. "Nike Is the Most Valuable Apparel Brand in the World." Nytimes.com. The New York Times, 29 May 2015. Web. 3 Dec. 2016.

H&M. "About » H&M Design Award 2017." H&M Design Award 2017 About Comments. H&M, 2016. Web. 15 Nov. 2016.

MailOnline, Gemma Mullin. "New Blow to Topshop as High Court Rules Store Must Pay Rihanna's 'startling' £1.5million Legal Bill Racked up When She Won Ban on Fashion Chain Using Her Picture on T-shirt."

Mail Online. Associated Newspapers, 03 Feb. 2015. Web. 13 Nov. 2016.

O'Connor, Clare. "Bethany Mota, Maria Sharapova On How To Build A Brand When There Are No Blueprints." Forbes. Forbes Magazine, 18 Oct. 2016. Web. 04 Dec. 2016.

Orange Technical College. Catalog, 2016-2017. Orlando: Orange Technical College, 2016. Catalog. Orange Technical College, 2016. Web. Nov. 2016.

Salvatore Ferragamo. Salvatore Ferragamo Launches First Online Trunk Show. Salvatore Ferragamo, 3 Aug. 2011. Web. 23 Nov. 2016.

Score Association. "SCORE | Free Small Business Advice." SCORE | Free Small Business Advice. Score Association, 2016. Web. 05 Dec. 2016.

Selfridges & Co. "Gucci Pop Up At Selfridges London." Selfridges. Selfridges & Co., 29 Jan. 2016. Web. 5 Dec. 2016.

Siegel + Gale. Logos Now. Rep. Siegel + Gale, 2015. Web. 4 Dec. 2016.

Stella & Dot LLC. "About Us." Stelladot.com. Stella & Dot LLC, 2016. Web. 23 Nov. 2016.

University of Arts London, Web Team. "Portfolio Advice." London College of Fashion. N.p., 2016. Web. 15 Nov. 2016.

Glossary

Acetate: A manmade fiber created from cellulose. It's very versatile and resistant to shrinking.

Acrylic: A manmade fiber created from long chain synthetic polymers. First created by the Dupont Corporation in 1941. Warm, dry, and wrinkle-resistant.

Adobe Illustrator: Computer software marketed by Adobe Systems that can create vector graphics for any medium. Useful for creating logos, patterns, or designs that maintain detail and proportion regardless of size.

Alterationist: Someone who adjusts store-bought garments to create a better fit. Not the same as a tailor, who custom-makes a garment to customer specifications.

Apparel Engineer: Someone who analyzes quality, efficiency, and productivity in garment manufacturing, and seeks to maximize all three through the creation and implementation of procedures.

Assistant Buyer: Buyers research trends, visit clothing suppliers, and generally decide what items their employer will sell. Assistant buyers help with research, filing, and paperwork, and generally assist the buyer in their decision-making.

Association of Sewing Design Professionals: An association of approximately 400 members who are involved in sewing and design-related businesses of all sizes. They host a national conference, and offer a master certification program.

Balance: Describes how evenly the visual weight of a garment is distributed. Usually balanced from left to right, not top to bottom.

Bellows: A type of pleat, typically seen on the sides of pockets (sometimes called "safari pockets") common on utility vests or jackets. The bellows allows for expansion of the depth of the pocket.

Blind Stitch: A method of stitching where the thread is nearly invisible on one or both sides of the fabric.

Blog: A regularly updated website written in a conversational or informal tone.

Boutique: A small, fashionable store that serves a specialized clientele.

Box pleat: Two equal folds of fabric, facing away from each other, and running parallel to one another. Commonly seen on pockets, drapery treatments, and bed skirts.

Branding: The process of linking your products to certain images or words, so consumers can differentiate between your competitors and you.

Broadcloth: A plain woven cloth, typically made of cotton or a cotton blend. Broadcloth is dense, durable, and of a heavier weight than standard cotton cloth.

Business License: To sell products, you may need a city or county business license. If you will buy tax-exempt, wholesale supplies, you need to have a business license number. In addition, you need this number to file sales tax on any goods you sell locally.

Business Plan: Formal, written document that explains how a business will run. It covers the financial, operational, and marketing details, and future goals of the business.

Butcher's Linen: Heavy bleached linen, similar to the texture of canvas, which is commonly used for aprons and tablecloths.

Care Labeling Rule: Set by the Federal Trade Commission. Textile wearing apparel or piece goods that are used to make wearing apparel are required to have permanent labels with clear instructions on how to wash, dry, and press them to maintain their appearance and quality. Some accessories like shoes, gloves, hats, and belts are exempt.

Challis: Lightweight woven fabric, usually a blend of cotton and silk, and sometimes incorporating a floral pattern.

China Silk: Very smooth, lustrous, plain silk that is mostly produced in China. Commonly used for linings, lingerie, and some summer blouses.

Clientele: Your customers.

Color Theory: Defines or categorizes colors based on the color wheel, and can guide you in combining or contrasting them to achieve different effects.

Computer Aided Design or Drafting (CAD): Using specialized computer software to create detailed blueprints or patterns for 3D objects. Useful for patternmakers, or designers who contract out the manufacturing of their clothing line.

Consignment: When retailers display a designer's clothing for a set period of time or until it is sold. You still own the clothing, and you receive payment when it is purchased. The retailer and the designer each get a percentage of the sale price.

Contrast: The concept of two closely associated items being different from each other, to varying degrees.

Copyright: The legal property rights to an original creative work. The owner can publish, reproduce, and sell the work. A piece is automatically protected from the moment it is created until 70 years after the creator's death.

Corporation: A business that is legally separate from its owners, and owned by stockholders.

Costume: Clothing intended for a specific use, as in a play or to celebrate a holiday. Typically represents a geographical region, or historical period.

Cotton: A soft white fiber that surrounds the seeds of the cotton plant, and that is used as a textile fiber and thread.

Couture: Term used to describe high-fashion, custom-made formal wear.

Crepe: Fabric (made of natural or synthetic fibers) that has a crisp or crimped appearance.

Customer Service: Any procedure or interaction that affects a customer's experience with your business.

Damask: A heavy fabric with a pattern that is visible on both sides. Usually used to make drapery and upholstery.

Dart: A pointed fold stitched into a garment to allow the flat fabric to take on a shape more suited to the curves of a human body.

Design Assistant: Someone who supports a fashion designer to create new materials, styles, colors, and patterns.

Distribution: Getting your product to consumers. In a small business you can do this directly, but for large businesses it's cheaper to hire a company that specializes in the distribution of manufactured goods to retail chains.

Doing Business As (DBA): The name a company operates under, which may differ from its legal name. For example, if you run a sole proprietorship and you want the business to have a name other than just your name, you would file for a DBA certificate as "Jane Doe DBA Jane's Jackets."

Donegal: A woven tweed (rough woolen fabric) with colorful yarn slubs (irregularities) throughout. Typically used for suiting, winter coats, and caps. Traditionally made in County Donegal, Ireland.

Drop Feed: A type of sewing machine that sews a straight stitch through lightweight to medium-weight fabrics.

Duck: A heavy, plain woven cotton fabric commonly known as "canvas."

Dupioni: A type of silk woven with uneven thread that has small slubs running horizontally through the weave.

Ebay: One of the internet's largest auction sites.

Etsy: An online marketplace for entrepreneurs to sell unique items that they make or curate.

Facing: A small piece of fabric, not necessarily matching the main fabric of the piece, used to give edges a finished look. Typically used on necklines, arm holes, hems, and other openings in garments.

Faille: A type of silk woven with a slight ribbed pattern and commonly used to make formal dresses.

Fashion Show: Designers hire models to parade their clothing line through a gauntlet of photographers, journalists, and possible customers. Fashion shows give buyers or consumers a chance to see your line, and give you the opportunity to see the response to your new designs.

Federal Trade Commission: An agency of the United States government that is charged with protecting consumers from predatory business practices.

Felt: A type of fabric made by matting and compressing wool or acrylic fibers together.

Finished Drawing: Used for presentations or publications. They show the style, line, and texture of the outfit and should be consistent with the designer company's image.

Flannel: A loosely-woven fabric, usually made of wool or cotton, that is brushed on one or both sides to create a soft texture. Often used for cold-weather clothing and sheets.

Focal point: A detail on a garment (beading, embroidery, hardware, etc.) that draws the viewer's eye to a certain area of the garment.

Form: The shape and structure of a garment. The form of a piece of clothing can be hard to describe with a single sketch, so designers may draw the garment from several angles.

Gabardine: A durable twill fabric, made of natural or synthetic fibers, that is normally used to make jackets or heavier items of clothing.

Garment Manufacturing License: In some states you may need this license to comply with local laws regarding the manufacturing of clothing.

Georgette: A lightweight, sheer material made of silk or crepe that is usually used to make dresses or blouses.

Grader's Set Square: A staple of the designer's toolkit, the set square is a guide for drawing geometric shapes like squares and rectangles, but it's also helpful when resizing patterns or adding seam allowances to a design.

Grading: Resizing a pattern.

Hand: The hand of a garment is a description of how it drapes and flows when touched. Hand is more than texture; it includes the weight and thickness of the fabric, the fibers used, and the tightness of the weave.

Hobbyist Equipment: Equipment sold to the general public that may not be as durable or have as many features as equipment meant for professional use.

Incorporation Fees: You will have to file paperwork with the federal and state government to become a corporation. There are fees associated with the filing, which may vary from state to state.

Instagram: A social media application that allows people to share captioned photos of whatever they like. People can follow each other or businesses to keep up on current trends and find inspiration.

Insurance: Business insurance policies cover you financially in the event of damage, loss, illness, or even death.

Intellectual Property: A work, invention, or idea for which a person may apply for a patent, copyright, or trademark. Think Snoopy, Lady Gaga, or the Dallas Cowboys.

Interfacing: Fabric used to line a garment for a certain purpose, such as to stiffen a soft fabric for a shirt collar, strengthen buttonholes, or keep knit fabrics from losing their shape.

International Apparel Federation, The: An association of retailers, brands, and manufacturers that seeks to maximize the value of global cooperation in the apparel industries.

International Woolmark Prize: A fashion award given by The Woolmark Company, a subsidiary of the not-for-profit Australian Wool Innovation enterprise, for showcasing the beauty of Merino wool.

Internship: A temporary job, paid or unpaid, that allows you to learn on-the-job.

Jersey: Knit fabric made from cotton or cotton blends. Commonly used to make t-shirts.

Junior Visual Merchandiser: Visual merchandisers use attractive retail displays to engage customers and increase sales.

Kiosk: A small mobile cart or hut that is used to sell retail items. Seen in shopping malls or anywhere people gather.

Knife pleat: Folds of fabric are pressed in the same direction. Commonly used in tuxedo shirts and kilts.

Licensing Agreement: A legal contract that allows a designer to use another person's copyrighted, trademarked, or patented material in their own goods, in exchange for royalties or a fee.

Limited Liability Corporation: Combines the characteristics of a corporation and sole proprietorship. Legally separates the company's members and owners from the company itself, so they cannot be held personally responsible for the company's debts or liabilities.

Line: 1) Term used to describe a designer's body of work. 2) The two-dimensional representation of a garment that can be boiled down to one or a combination of geometric shapes.

Linen: Fabric made from the fiber of the flax plant. It is lightweight and cool in hot weather, and stronger than cotton, but it wrinkles easily due to a lack of elasticity.

Lining: Fabric used on the inside of a garment to give it body, help it retain its shape, and make the garment more comfortable as a design element under a sheer fabric, etc.

Linker: A machine that can join knitted fabric together easily and quickly, with a high degree of accuracy (very important in the case of patterned or striped fabric).

Logo: A symbol or design used to designate a brand.

Look Book: A direct marketing tool that you can send to boutique owners and buyers for chain stores. You should produce a look book each season to showcase your current collection.

Mackinaw: Heavy, dense, and water-repellent cloth made of wool, typically used to make jackets of the same name.

MailChimp: A leading email-marketing platform that allows businesses to send emails, automated messages, and targeted campaigns to clients.

Manmade Fibers: Can be made of cellulose or petroleum. Rayon is a cellulose-based fiber. Nylon is a petroleum product. Petroleum-based fibers are also called synthetic fibers.

Manufacturing: The process of physically creating or building your products.

Marketing: The art of convincing customers to choose your designs over your competitors'.

Matelasse: Fabric (often silk) with a raised design that gives it the appearance of having been quilted.

Muslin: Plain cotton weaves of various thicknesses.

Nap: The raised or fuzzy surface on some types of cloth, such as velvet or flannel.

Natural Fibers: Come from animals (wool, mohair, alpaca) or plants (hemp, cotton).

Needle Feed: A type of sewing machine that sews a straight stitch through heavier fabrics.

Niche: In business, a niche is wherever a special interest intersects with basic needs. People *need* clothing of no specific design, but they *want* clothing that reflects their personality and interests.

Noil: Short fibers leftover from combing wool or spinning silk. Can be used as a decorative additive for other projects.

Notions: The various tools, parts, and products that are necessary for the act of sewing.

Nylon: A synthetic fabric made from petroleum products and developed as an alternative to silk. It is lightweight, strong, and durable, and was used extensively during WWII.

Oatmeal Cloth: A heavy but soft fabric with a speckled or uneven surface. Normally used for upholstery and drapery.

Ordering: As a designer, you will order many supplies to create your fashion line. Your customers will place orders with you, via any of a number of methods, for the garments you manufacture.

Organdy: Thin, transparent cloth made of cotton that is treated to give it varying degrees of stiffness. Typically used for women's clothing.

Organza: Similar to organdy, but made of silk or synthetic fibers instead of cotton. Typically used in evening-wear.

Partnership: A partnership offers the convenience of a sole proprietorship with the ability to share the ownership and responsibilities of the business with someone else. Like sole proprietorships, the parties involved in a partnership are personally responsible for any business debts.

Patternmaking: The act of creating the pattern by which a garment will be manufactured.

Payment: Obviously, you are required to make payment for your supplies and overhead costs. Your customers will pay you, via any of a number of methods, for the garments they purchase from you.

PayPal: A payment system that allows customers to pay for products without providing the business with their private credit card or bank information.

Peau de Soie: Silk fabric with a weight and feel similar to satin, but more structured or stiff. Has thin cross-ribs and a corded appearance. Used for formalwear.

Petite: Term used to describe any person who is 5'4" or under. Designs for petite women have different lines and cuts than patterns for taller clients.

Pinterest: A social media application that allows people to create a virtual collage or pin-board of anything that they like. People can follow each other or businesses to keep up on current trends and find inspiration.

Pleat: A design element created by folding and pressing or stitching fabric in various ways.

Plus size: Term used to describe any person who requires larger-sized clothing. There is no set standard for where the line falls, though for women it's somewhere between 12 and 16, and for juniors anything above a 13.

Polyester: A synthetic fabric made from synthesized polymers (which can also be made into recyclable plastic drink bottles). It's resilient and resistant to biological damage, but it's highly flammable.

Pongee: A thin silk fabric with a rough texture, used to make women's clothing.

Poplin: Woven cotton fabric with a slight ribbed texture, suitable for making shirts, dresses, or skirts.

Pop-up Shop: A retail space that opens without advertising, stays open for a few days or weeks, and then closes without warning.

Portfolio: Like a resume, but for fashion design. It's an ever-changing collection of your best sketches and looks, but should also represent your interests and inspiration, and include any experimentation or development of ideas that showcase your creativity.

Press Release: A way of announcing news and events to the media that is written in a standardized format.

Pricing: Pricing your clothes, taking into consideration the cost of materials, the amount of time involved in designing, the price of making the patterns and samples, and the manufacturing expenses for each individual piece. A common retail pricing strategy is to multiply the material and manufacturing costs of each style by 2.2 to 2.8.

Production: See "manufacturing."

Project Runway: Junior: An American reality television show that features fashion designers between the ages of 13 and 17. Based on Project Runway, which is for adult designers.

Proportion: The size of component pieces, as they relate to each other.

Publicity: Promoting your business to the public by hosting events, and using advertising and media to your best advantage.

Quality: The degree of excellence of a thing, as measured against other similar things.

Quick Pose: A type of fashion drawing used to show ideas to clients or collaborators. May be representative of the seeds of an idea, and not nearly as detailed as a finished drawing.

Ramie: A flowering plant from the nettle family, the bark of which is processed into a fiber and then into a fabric. It is strong but not durable, so is often blended with cotton or wool.

Rayon: A semi-synthetic fiber created from naturally occurring polymers. It is a versatile fiber, and there are several types of rayon that can imitate the feel and texture of silk, wool, cotton, or linen, though it has some properties similar to nylon.

Registered Identification Number (RN): Number issued to garment or textile manufacturers by the Federal Trade Commission. Your garment or textile label is required to have the RN number of the manufacturer on it. You can apply for an RN through the FTC.

Rendering: Coloring in a finished fashion drawing.

Resale License: License issued by a state to anyone wishing to sell products within their jurisdiction.

Retail: Selling your products directly to consumers.

Returns: Customers may occasionally be unsatisfied with items they've purchased from you, for any one of a variety of reasons, and they will want to return the item to you. You will have to determine a policy for returns, make it available to your customers prior to their purchase, and stick to it.

Rhythm: The pattern of the fabric you choose and the placement of details across the garment help guide the viewer's eye. The way people look across a piece, where their eyes linger, and what parts they skip, create the rhythm of the outfit.

Royalties: As part of a licensing agreement, in return for you allowing another person or company to use your intellectual property to sell products, you receive a percentage of the sale price of each item sold.

Ruffle: A strip of fabric, gathered on one edge and sewn onto a garment or other textile as a form of decoration.

Sample Garment: The first physical copy of a design. Allows you to see your design in three dimensions, on a model, and determine if the pattern needs to be altered in any way.Also helps you estimate the expense of producing it.

Sateen: A cotton fabric made to imitate satin by using a similar weave construction, it's glossy on the front and dull on the back.

SBA Microloan Program: The Small Business Administration's program for loans of less than $35,000, and which includes training and help for the business owner.

SCORE: A nonprofit resource partner of the Small Business Administration, they match new small business owners with volunteer mentors, and they offer free online materials and workshops.

Seamstress: A woman who makes a living by sewing. See also "tailor."

Search Engine Optimization (SEO): Using keywords and popular terms to ensure that your website appears in the list when someone searches for it on the internet.

Seconded: Items that are sold at a discount due to an error, such as a broken zipper, or a manufacturing or fabric defect.

Serger: A type of sewing machine that creates a finished, trimmed seam by cutting away excess fabric as it sews.

Silk: A strong, soft, and shiny fabric produced by collecting and processing silkworm cocoons into thread.

Silk Linen: Plain silk in a linen-type weave, with nubby crosshatches in both directions.

Slub: A lump or thick spot in a yarn or thread.

Small Business Association (SBA): A government agency that offers loans, contracts, counseling, and other forms of assistance to small businesses.

Snapchat: A social media application using image messaging, where the images are short-lived and self-deleting.

Sole Proprietorship: If you do not file any paperwork with the government, your business is a sole proprietorship. This means that any profits from the business are your personal income and are subject to income tax. You are responsible for paying all expenses for the business.

Sourcing: Finding the materials you need to build your garments.

Squarespace: A hosting system that allows individuals and businesses to create and maintain websites and blogs.

Storyboard: A collage to help you organize the ideas and inspiration behind a particular garment or line of garments.

Tailor: A man who makes a living by sewing. See also "seamstress."

Tartan: A woolen cloth woven in a plaid pattern, especially of a design associated with particular Scottish clans.

Technical (or Performance) Fibers or Fabrics: Created from synthetic fibers or natural/synthetic blends. May be knit or woven to bring out specific qualities, usually related to how the fiber manages heat or water.

Terry Cloth: Very absorbent cotton fabric with raised uncut loops of thread on both sides. Used for towels.

Textile and Wool Acts, The: A government regulation that ensures customers know what they are purchasing, and requires labels listing the fiber content, country of origin, and product manufacturer for the individual item.

Texture: Texture refers to the surface quality of the garment. The texture of a fabric is the result of the fibers used to create the fabric and the technique used to weave or knit it.

Trade Dress: Refers to the overall look of a product or its packaging that distinguishes and identifies the product, such as the distinctive blue box used by Tiffany & Co.

Trade Show: An exhibition organized for the benefit of companies in a specific industry. Showcases new technology, products, or services.

Trademark: A trademark is a word, name, symbol, or device used to distinguish a product from similar items. A product or process itself is not trademarked. The name, logo, or slogan that identifies the product is the trademark.

Trademark Registration: The process of registering your name, logo, or slogan with the United States Patent and Trademark Office.

Trend: The general direction in which something develops or changes.

Trunk Show: A party, at someone's home or in a rented space, where you display your sample garments directly to interested shoppers.

Tweed: A woolen fabric with a rough texture, typically with flecks of many colors incorporated into the weave.

Twill: A style of weaving that creates diagonal parallel ridges.

United States Patent and Trademark Office: A federal agency that grants patents and trademarks to protect ideas and investments in innovation and creativity.

Unity: Refers to the connection between the different pieces of the garment. One way to create unity in your design is through repetition. You can repeat patterns, textures, and colors throughout a piece. Unity helps create a sense that the design is intentional.

Venise: Damask linen featuring a floral pattern and made out of very fine threads.

Vent: A vertical slit starting at the hem of a skirt or jacket that allows for ease of movement.

Vlog: A video blog.

Walking Foot: A sewing machine that can sew a straight stitch through very thick or heavy fabrics.

Wholesale: Selling large quantities of items at a lower price to retailers, like stores who will sell the individual items to the customer.

Wix: A web development platform that allows users to create websites with user-friendly drag-and-drop tools. Registration and website building is free, but users must pay to connect their site(s) to the internet, add capabilities, upgrade data storage, etc.

Wool: The fine hair from the coat of a sheep or goat that is combed and spun into yarn or made into cloth.

Working Drawing: Used to show the details of a garment's construction to the pattern cutter.

Workmanship: The quality of the garment in terms of how it is constructed. Depending on the complexity of a style, there may be many places where manufacturing errors can occur. For example, the hem of a skirt might hang awkwardly, a zipper on a pair of pants might not stay up, or there might be missing stitches in a seam.

YouTube: A video-sharing website where subscribers can upload, view, rate, share, report, and comment on video clips of various types. Non-subscription users can view most videos, but cannot use any of the other features.

Zig Zag: A sewing machine that allows for side-to-side motion in addition to a straight stitch.

Index

About the Author

Lisa McGinnes is a writer and magazine editor who enjoys exploring the natural world in her kayak and on her mountain bike.

An alumna of Western Michigan University, she studied public relations and journalism. Lisa has experience in print and broadcast journalism, and has worked with several nonprofit organizations as a public relations and fundraising specialist.

Lisa and her husband love living in Florida, where they can have year-round outdoor adventures.

THE NEW SCHOOL
PARSONS *teen*VOGUE

Don't Just Follow Fashion. Define It.

Fashion Industry Essentials is a new online fashion program from the Parsons School of Fashion and Teen Vogue that teaches you everything you want to know about the business of fashion.

Taught by elite faculty from Parsons School of Design, *Teen Vogue* editors, and industry experts like Rebecca Minkoff, Brandon Maxwell, Elaine Welteroth, and Phillip Picardi, this program and certificate will help you get started in the global fashion industry.

So You Want to Be a Fashion Designer: Here's the Info You Need readers can receive a $100 tuition discount to this program by using promo code **PTVFashion** when you enroll at: **http://teenvogue.parsons.edu/bookoffer**.